Enrich You
WORDS AND

BOOKS IN ENGLISH LANGUAGE LEARNING SERIES

Grammer Matters

Common Errors in English

Dictionary for Misspellers

Idioms

Quotations

Proverbs

Riddles

Tongue Twisters

The Complete Guide to

Business Letters

Effective English Writing

Essays for Competitive Examinations

Functional Writing in English

Modern Essays

Paragraph to Essay Writing

Prose Compositions

Résumé Writing

Letters for Social Interaction

Enrich your Grammar

Antonyms

Current Words and Phrases

Prepositions

Synonyms

Word Perfect

Word Power

Word to Paragraph

Words and Their Usages

Word Origins

Communications Skills

The Power of Spoken English (with 2 audio CDs)

Speaking and Writing in English

Dynamic Reading Skills

Effective Communication

English Conversation Practice

How to Develop Profitable Listening Skills

How to Increase Your Reading Speed

How to Listen Better

How to Read Effectively and Efficiently

How to Resolve Conflicts

Enrich Your Grammar
WORDS AND THEIR USAGES

DR MAHESWAR PANDA

M.A., Ph.D.
Reader & Head, Deptt. of English,
J.K.B.K. College, Cuttack

A Sterling Paperback

STERLING PAPERBACKS
An imprint of
Sterling Publishers (P) Ltd.
A-59, Okhla Industrial Area, Phase-II,
New Delhi-110020.
Tel: 26387070, 26386209; Fax: 91-11-26383788
E-mail: sterlingpublishers@airtelbroadband.in
ghai@nde.vsnl.net.in
www.sterlingpublishers.com

Words and Their Usages

ISBN 978 81 207 2006 0
Reprint 2008

Printed and Published by Sterling Publishers Pvt. Ltd.,
New Delhi-110 020.

CONTENTS

PREFACE

"First of all, I tell you earnestly and authoritatively (I know I am right) you must get into the habit of looking intensely at words, and assuring yourself of their meaning, syllable by syllable, nay, letter by letter."

—*John Ruskin*

(The object of this small book, as the title implies, is to concentrate on the right use of certain words in our everyday speech and writing of English. In writing this book, my sole aim has been to help the learner towards his own understanding of the grammatically appropriate use of words in various contexts in his speech and writing. It is basically an aid to be used like any dictionary, to be consulted and then put aside. Since it does not set out to be a full-length treatment of traditional grammar, I have been constrained to reduce the contents of the book solely with a view to meeting the long-felt requirements of the students studying in various colleges of Indian Universities and of those preparing for various competitive examinations).

Words are the basic components of a language and as such an understanding of its function is of paramount importance. It is a fact that an English course for an Indian student must necessarily concentrate on the structure of the language. But then, a knowledge of how to use appropriate words in the correct context is also vitally important. The book is designed to provide systematic practice in the use of words in one's speech and writing. Words are lowest in the order of linguistic composition. A word that is not grammatically appropriate in its use to the context, a loose phrase, an ambiguous expression, a vague adjective, will not satisfy a learner who aims at clean and correct English. He will apply his effort to using the word that is completely right for his purpose.

Adequate attention has been paid to the selection of items included in this volume chiefly from a practical point of view for fulfilling the needs of the learner for whom English is a foreign language. The first item focuses attention on the formation of compound and derivative words from the 'root' words and shows how new words can be formed by adding prefixes and suffixes to the words. The second deals with the right arrangement of words in a sentence. The rules governing it have been set forth and ample illustrations have been provided to make the learner understand them. The third chapter deals with compound words and their meanings. A list of such words as can be expanded into equivalent phrases by using appropriate prepositions to connect the words of which they are formed, has also been given. The fourth chapter sets forth an exhaustive list of single words for groups of words and attempts to show that there is no need to use a group of words when a single word conveys their meanings. In the fifth chapter, an attempt has been made to show the difference in meaning between similar words. There are some words which look similar in spelling and pronunciation but are entirely different in meaning from each other. Adequate care has been taken to distinguish the one from the other by using them in sentences. There are also some words which can be used both as nouns and verbs and such words used like this have been shown in sentences. This has been dealt with exhaustively in the sixth chapter. Chapter seven makes an extensive use of appropriate prepositions after certain words. Since there are no hard and fast rules to guide the learner properly in his use of prepositions after certain parts of speech, he has to cultivate the habit of reading and using them time and again. Chapter eight, which deals with the use of idioms and phrases in sentences, is certainly an important item of grammar since idiomatic English lends a good deal of charm to the effectiveness of expression and meaning. It consists of a succession of words for which the meaning must be understood as a whole. Idiomatic English helps the learner develop a good style of writing and as such a cautious use of it is necessary lest it should confound the learner or tend to be artificial and stiff. Chapter nine treats punctuation, stops or points which are a vital part of written/spoken languages. There are certain signs which indicate speech pauses and without them our meaning would not always be clearly understood. In the tenth chapter, an attempt has been made to show the structural difference and similarity in meaning between phrases and clauses. Phrases used in sentences have been converted to clauses, keeping the meaning identical in both cases. Phrases and clauses have been analysed and the underlying differences in the construction of sentences and in their meaning being identical , have been demonstrated clearly through illustrative examples. Chapter eleven indicates the rules governing spelling which is an important part of written language. The learner, owing to his carelessness in spelling of words, tends to commit errors. A thorough acquaintance with the rules is, therefore, highly essential. In chapter twelve, an exhaustive list of words has been given to acquaint the learner with their antonyms and synonyms. All that is required of him is to grow accustomed to remembering these words with their contrary and identical meanings respectively. In chapters thirteen and fourteen, which form the concluding part of this book, some words used as inchoative verbs and such courtesy words as 'Please' and 'Thank you' and certain words used for 'greetings and salutations' have been dealt with from a practical point of view. Sometimes the learner is likely to make mistakes in the use of these words in sentences and so ample illustrations have been provided to draw his attention to the appropriate use of them in various contexts.

At the end of each chapter, exercises have been given to enable the learner to test his comprehension of what he has learnt and remembered.

The author is thankful to the publisher for taking so much interest in bringing out this educationally useful book.

I hope the students will find this book useful.

Cuttack

M. PANDA

1
FORMATION OF WORDS

Words which are neither derived nor compounded nor even developed from other words are called Simple or Primary words. They come from the original stock of words in the language. Such words as moon, bare, take, etc., are some of the Simple or Primary words from which many other words can be formed. Such words are also called 'Roots'. There are two kinds of words formed out of Simple or Primary words. They are (i) Compound words, and (ii) Derivatives or Derived words. A Compound word can be formed by joining two or more Primary words so as to make one; as, moonlight (moon+light), barefoot (bare+foot), undertake (under+take), doorstep (door+step), ink-pot (ink+pot), drinking water (drinking + water), etc. (see Chapter 3)

Derivatives or derived words can be formed by making some change in the body of the Primary words by means of the internal changes such as, 'bond' from 'bind', 'feed' from 'food', 'song' from 'sing' and also by adding a letter or group of letters at the beginning or at the end of the Primary word such as, 'unkind' from 'kind', 'reclaim' from 'claim', 'manhood' from 'man', 'fortunate' from 'fortune', etc.

There are many derivatives in English which are formed by the addition of syllables to the Primary words. These syllables are to be placed either at the beginning or at the end of the Primary words to modify their meaning. The syllable used at the beginning of a Primary word is called a 'prefix' and the syllable used at the end of a Primary word is called a 'suffix'. A list of a few prefixes and suffixes that can be grouped together to form different words is presented here.

i) Prefixes and suffixes used to form *Transitive Verbs from Nouns or Adjectives:*

Prefixes:

Be   : Bedew, befriend, behead, belittle.

En-, em, im- : Endear, enslave, enable, embowel, empower, imperial, improper, immoderate, immobile, etc.

Suffixes:

-en   : Darken, hasten, lengthen, lighten, sweeten, etc.

-fy   : Beautify, purify, simplify, horrify, terrify, etc.

-ize or ise   : civilize, moralise, realize, mobilize, etc.

ii) Prefixes and suffixes used to form negatives:

Prefixes:

A-, an-   : Apathy, atheist, anarchy, anomalous.

Dis-   : Disadvantage, disallow, disability, disabuse, disaffected, disagree, disappear, disappoint, disapprobation, disapprove, disarm, disarray, disavow, disbelieve, disbud, disburden, discolour, discomfort, disconsolate, discontent, discontinue, discount, discourage, discourteous, discredit, disembarrass, disembody, disembowel, disembroil, disencumber, disentangle, disestablish, disfigure, disfavour, disforest, disfranchise, disgrace, disguise, dishonest, dishonour, disillusion, disincentive, disincline, disinfected, disinflation, disingenuous, disinherit, disintegrate, disinterested, disjoint, dislike, dislocate, dislodge, dismantle, disobey, disorder, disorganise, disown, dispassionate, displace, display, displeasure, dispossess, disproportion, disprove, disqualify, disquiet, disregard, disrelish, disrespect, dissemble, disservice, dissimilar, dissimulate, dissoluble, disunion, disuse.

For -   : Forwards, forbid, forlorn, forbear, forearm, forgive, forfeit, forgather, forget, forsake, forswear, forecast, forebode, forecastle, foreclose, forecourt, foredown, forefathers, forefinger, forefoot, forego, foreground, forehead, forehand, foreknow, foreland, foreleg, forelock, foreman, foremost, forename, forenoon, foreordain, forepart, forerunner, foresee, foreshadow, foreshore, foresight, forestall, foretaste, foretell, forethought, forewarn.

In-, it,
im-, ir- : Inability, inaccessible, inaccurate, inaction, inadequate, inadmissible, inalienable, inapplicable, inappreciable, inappropriate, inapt, inarticulate, inattention, inaudible, inauspicious, inborn, inbred, incalculable, incapable, incapacitate, incertitude, incoming, incomparable, incomprehensive, inconceivable, inconclusive, incongruous, inconsequential, inconsiderable, inconsistent, inconsolable, inconstant, inconspicuous, incontestable, incontrovertible, inconvenience, inconvertible, incorporate, incorrect, incorruptible, incredible, incurable, indebted, indecent, indecisive, indecorum, indefinite, indelible, indelicate, independent, indescribable, indeterminate, indifference, indigestion, indignity, indirect, indiscipline, indiscreet, indiscriminate, indisposed, indisputable, indissoluble, indistinct, indivisible, indoctrinate, indoor, indwelling, inedible, ineffable, ineffective, inefficient, ineligible, inequality, ineradicable, inestimable, inevitable, inexact, inexcusable, inexhaustible, inexpensive, inexorable, inexplicable, inexpressible, inextinguishable, inextricable, infallible, infamous, inflame, inflow, influx, informal, ingress, inhabit, inharmonious, inhere, inhospitable, inhuman, injudicious, injustice, inland, in-laws, inlay, inlet, inmate, inmost, inoffensive, inoperable, inopportune, inorganic, input, inrush, insatiable, inside, insincere, insubstantial, insupportable, insurmountable, intake, intangible, intemperate, intractable, intransitive, invalid, invaluable,

inviolable, invisible, inward, illegal, illegitimate, illuminate, immoral, immovable, immoderate, irregular, irradiate, irrational, irreconciliable, irrecoverable, irredeemable, irreducible, irrefutable, irrelevant, irreligious, irremediable, irremovable, irreparable, irreplaceable, irrepressible, irreproachable, irresistible, irresolute, irrespective, irresponsible, irretrievable, irreverent, irrevocable.

N-   : None, never, neither, nor.

Non-   : Nonsense.

Un -   : Unhappy, unsafe, unable, unabated, unaccountable, unaccustomed, unadopted unadvised, unaffected, unalterable, unannounced, unanswerable, unapproachable, unarmed, unasked, unassuming, unattached, unattended, unavailing, unavoidable, unaware, unbalanced, unbearable, unbeaten, unbecoming, unbelief, unbend, unbiased, unblushing, unbosom, unbounded, unbowed, unbridled, unbroken, unburden, uncalled, uncanny, unceasing, uncertain, uncharitable, uncharted, unchecked, unchristian, uncivil, unclaimed, unclouded, unclean, uncoloured, uncommitted, uncommon, uncompromising, unconcerned, uncouple, uncover, uncrossing, unconsidered, unconditional, unconscious, uncut, undaunted, undeceive, undefended, undemonstrative, undeniable.

Suffix:

- less   : Careless, aimless, doubtless, dauntless, fathomless, faithless, formless, guiltless, homeless, helpless, hopeless, lawless, motionless, etc.

iii) There are certain prefixes which are used to show the reversal or undoing of something done:

De-   : Delink, devoid, dethrone, decamp, detach, devitalise, dehumanised, derecognise.

Dis -   : Dismantle, dislocate, disallow, dismember, disintegrate, dismount, disappear, disinterested, dishonest, disavowal, disfavour, disarm.

Un - : Unfold, unlock, untie.

The following is a list of some important *suffixes* which are used in the formation of new words:

a) To form *Abstract Nouns* indicating state, action, condition, etc.:

- age : bondage, marriage.
- ance, -ence : abundance, excellence.
- acy, -cy : accuracy, bankruptcy.
- dom : freedom, wisdom.
- hood : boyhood, manhood, childhood.
- ice : cowardice, justice.
- ion : action, rebellion.
- ism : criticism, patriotism.
- ment : imprisonment, punishment.
- ness : darkness, sweetness.
- red : hatred.
- ry, -ery : slavery, treachery.
- ship : hardship, friendship.
- sion : admission, compulsion.
- tion : reduction, translation.
- th : growth, health.
- tude : aptitude, servitude.
- ty, - ity : cruelty, reality.
-y : misery, victory.

b) To form *Nouns* naming an agent or doer:

-ain, -an, -en : chieftain, captain, artisan, citizen.
-ant, -ent : servant, student, president.
-ar, -er, -or : scholar, teacher, sailor.
-ary, -aire : missionary, millionaire.
-eer, -ier : engineer, financier.
-ee, -y : trustee, payee, deputy.
-ist : artist, chemist.
-ive : captive, native.
-ot : patriot, idiot.

c) To form *Verbs* :

i) *Transitive* -
-ate, -ize-or-ise, -ish : Captivate, civilize, finish.

ii) *Causative,* that is, showing causation of action.
-en, -fy : darken, simplify.

iii) *Frequentative,* that is, showing frequent repetition of action.
-er, -le, -l : flutter, dazzle, kneel.

    iv) *Intransitive:*
          -ate, -en, -ish : speculate, happen, flourish.
d) To form *Adjectives:*

-al	:	fatal, national, devotional.
-an,-ane	:	human, humane.
-ar	:	Lunar, familiar.
-ant, -ent:		ignorant, innocent.
-ary	:	customary, necessary.
-ate	:	accurate, fortunate.
-ble, -able		
-ible	:	feeble, lovable, sensible.
-ed	:	aged, gifted.
-en	:	wooden, silken, bounden.
-ern	:	eastern, northern, western, southern.
-ful	:	helpful, harmful, truthful, fearful.
-ian	:	Christian, Indian, Canadian, Australian, Egyptian, Mongolian, Scandinavian.
-ic	:	dramatic, heroic.
-ish	:	boyish, girlish, fiendish.
-ite	:	favourite, opposite, composite.
-ive	:	active, passive, relative, impressive, persuasive.
-less	:	careless, worthless, hopeless.
-ly	:	lovely, manly.
-ory	:	compulsory, transitory, illusory.
-ous	:	dangerous, glorious, barbarous, lecherous, treacherous, garrulous.
-some	:	tiresome, troublesome, quarrelsome, pointsome.
-ward	:	backward, forward, downward, inward, outward.
-y	:	dirty, thirsty, nasty, hasty, naughty.

e) To form *Adverbs:*

-ly	:	bravely, boldly, calmly, wisely.
-long	:	headlong, sidelong.
-wise	:	otherwise, likewise, suchwise.
-way,		
-ways	:	anyway, always.

f) *Diminutives:*

-el, -le	:	navel (nave), satchel (sack), freckle (freck), sparkle (spark).
-en	:	chicken (from cock), kitten (from cat), maiden.

-ing	:	farthing, tithing, shilling, whiting, wilding.
-ling	:	duckling, gosling, darling, nurseling, darkling, suckling, seedling, changeling, hireling, weakling.
-kin	:	lambkin, firkin, Peterkin or perkin, napkin.
-ock	:	hillock, bullock, paddock (from park), hammock (from hump).
-ie, -y	:	birdie, baby, lassie, daddy.

It is now clear that new words can be formed by adding prefixes and suffixes to the words. The following is a list of new words which indicate that nouns can be formed from verbs, and adjectives; abstract nouns from nouns; verbs from nouns and adjectives; adjectives from nouns and verbs, etc.:

(A)   (i) Formation of Nouns from Verbs.

Verbs	Nouns	Verbs	Nouns
Abound	Abundance	Exist	Existence
Admit	Admission	Expect	Expectation
Agree	Agreement	Expel	Expulsion
Amuse	Amusement	Free	Freedom
Apply	Application	Furnish	Furniture
Approve	Approval	Grow	Growth
Arrive	Arrival	Hate	Hatred
Assist	Assistance	Heal	Health
Attend	Attendance	Judge	Judgement
Attract	Attraction	Know	Knowledge
Bless	Blessing	Laugh	Laughter
Bury	Burial	Learn	Learning
Carry	Carriage	Manage	Management
Compel	Compulsion	Marry	Marriage
Conceal	Concealment	Mean	Meaning
Connect	Connection	Motion	Move
Deceive	Deception	Narrate	Narration
Decide	Decision		Narrative
Deliver	Deliverance	Obey	Obedience
	Delivery	Object	Objection
Deny	Denial	Occupy	Occupation
Discover	Discovery	Oppose	Opposition
Dismiss	Dismissal	Perform	Performance
Exceed	Excess	Please	Pleasure

Verbs	Nouns	Verbs	Nouns
Pretend	Pretence	Secure	Security
	Pretension	Seize	Seizure
Proceed	Procedure	Serve	Service
	Process	Slay	Slaughter
Protect	Protection	Steal	Stealth
Provide	Provision	Succeed	Success
Quote	Quotation	Try	Trial
Reduce	Reduction	Urge	Urgency
Refer	Reference	Vacate	Vacation
Refresh	Refreshment		Vacancy
Refuse	Refusal	Vary	Variety
Resolve	Resolution	Wed	Wedding
Respond	Response	Weigh	Weight
Reveal	Revelation	Write	Writing

(ii) Formation of Nouns from Adjectives.

Adjectives	Nouns	Adjectives	Nouns
Able	Ability	Free	Freedom
Abundant	Abundance	Gay	Gaiety
Active	Activity	Generous	Generosity
Brave	Bravery	Grand	Grandeur
Breadth	Brevity	Great	Greatness
Brief	Broad	Happy	Happiness
Busy	Business	Hard	Hardness
Calm	Calmness		Hardship
Certain	Certainty	High	Height
Cheap	Cheapness	Holy	Holiness
Civil	Civility	Honest	Honesty
Coward	Cowardice	Inferior	Inferiority
Curious	Curiosity	Just	Justice
Dense	Deep	Lame	Lameness
Depth	Density	Local	Locality
Equal	Equality	Long	Length
False	Falsehood	Mean	Meanness
Fast	Fastness	Merry	Merriment
	Falsity	Moist	Moisture
Fertile	Fertility	Mortal	Mortality
Frank	Frankness	Necessary	Necessity

Adjectives	Nouns	Adjectives	Nouns
New	Newness	Sacred	Sacredness
Noble	Nobility	Safe	Safety
Obedient	Obedience	Scarce	Scarcity
One	Oneness	Severe	Severity
Perfect	Perfection	Short	Shortage
Pious	Piety		Shortness
Popular	Popularity	Slow	Slowness
Poverty	Poor	Solitary	Solitude
	Pride	Special	Speciality
Privacy	Private	Splendid	Splendour
Proud	Prudence	Strong	Strength
	Prudent	Stupid	Stupidity
Pure	Purity	Supreme	Supremacy
Quick	Quickness	Sweet	Sweetness
Real	Reality	Timid	Timidity
Red	Redness	Vacant	Vacancy
Rich	Richness	Vain	Vanity
Rigid	Rigidity	Weak	Weakness
Rival	Rivalry	Wide	Width
Round	Roundness	Wise	Wisdom
Royal	Royalty	Young	Youth

iii) Formation of Abstract Nouns from Nouns.

Nouns	Abstract Nouns	Nouns	Abstract Nouns
Act	Action	Man	Manhood
Agent	Agency	Mother	Motherhood
Baby	Babyhood	Owner	Ownership
Beggar	Beggary	Patriot	Patriotism
Bond	Bondage	Priest	Priesthood
Child	Childhood	Regent	Regency
Coin	Coinage	Servant	Service
Creature	Creation	Slave	Slavery
Friend	Friendship	Teacher	Teachership
Hero	Heroism	Widow	Widowhood
Infant	Infancy	Woman	Womanhood
King	Kingship		

(B)(i) Formation of Verbs from Nouns.

Nouns	Verb	Nouns	Verb
Apology	Apologise	Harmony	Harmonise
Associate	Authority	Haste	Hasten
	Authorise	Head	Behead
Battle	Embattle	Heir	Inherit
Beauty	Beautify	Horror	Horrify
Black	Blacken	Idol	Idolise
Body	Embody	Peril	Imperil
Cage	Encage	Invigorate	Vijour
Camp	Encamp	Invigorate	Vitiate
Centre	Concentract	Justice	Justify
Character	Characterise	Knee	Kneel
Christ	Christen	Length	Lengthen
Cipher	Decipher	Magnet	Magnetise
Circle	Class	Mass	Amass
	Classify	Memory	Memorise
Colony	Colonise	Monopoly	Monopolise
Company	Accompany	Nation	Nationalise
	Concentrate	Nature	Naturalise
Courage	Encourage	Necessity	Necessitate
Critic	Criticise	Nest	Nestle
Danger	Endanger	Neuter	Neutralise
Decipher		Office	Officiate
Deity	Deify	Origin	Originate
Dew	Bedew	Peace	Pacify
Economy	Economise	Patron	Patronise
Electricity	Electrify	Person	Personate
Famine	Famish	Population	Populate
Force	Enforce	Power	Empower
Fool	Befool	Port	Export
Fraud	Defraud		Transport
Friend	Befriend		Import
Fright	Frighten	Prison	Imprison
Game	Gambol	Red	Redden
Glory	Glorify	Sermon	Sermonise
Guide	Beguile	Slave	Enslave
Habit	Habituate	Society	Associate
Hand	Handle	Spark	Sparkle

Nouns	Verb	Nouns	Verb
Substance	Substantiate	Title	Entitle
Sympathy	Sympathise	Tomb	Entomb
System	Systematise	Utility	Utilise
Table	Tabulate	Vapour	Evaporate
Terror	Terrify	Verse	Versify
Terrorise	Throne	Vice	Vigour
	Enthrone		

(i) Formation of Verbs from Adjectives.

Adjectives	Verb	Adjectives	Verb
Able	Enable	Fine	Refine
Alien	Alienate	General	Generalise
Ascertain	Ascertainable	Glad	Gladden
Base	Debase	Just	Justify
Bitter	Embitter	Low	Lower
Bold	Embolden	Mad	Madden
Brief	Abbreviate	Mean	Demean
Broad	Broaden	Moist	Moisten
Calm	Becalm	New	Renew
Certain	Ascertain	Perpetual	Perpetuate
Cheap	Cheapen	Poor	Impoverish
Civil	Civilise	Popular	Popularise
Clear	Clarify	Proper	Appropriate
Clean	Cleanse	Public	Publicise
Dark	Darken	Publish	Pure
Dear	Endear		Purify
Deep	Deepen	Rare	Rarefy
Dense	Condence	Real	Realise
Different	Differentiate	Right	Rectify
Double	Duplicate	Rich	Enrich
Enable	Endear	Sick	Sicken
Enfeeble	Enlarge	Solid	Consolidate
Ennoble	Enrich	Special	Specialise
Equal	Equalise	Specific	Specify
False	Falsify	Stabilise	Stable
Familiar	Familiarise	Strange	Estrange
Fertile	Fertlise	Sure	Ensure
Feeble	Enfeeble	Thick	Thicken

Adjectives	Verb	Adjectives	Verb
Timid	Intimidate	White	Whiten
Vile	Vilify	Wide	Widen

(C) (i)   Formation of Adjectives from Nouns.

Nouns	Adjectives	Nouns	Adjectives
Advantage	Advantageous	Chivalry	Chivalrous
Adventure	Adventurous	Circle	Circular
Accident	Accidental	Child	Childish,
Advice	Advisable		Childlike
Affection	Affectionate	Class	Classic,
Air	Airy		Classical
Ancestor	Ancestral	Colony	Colonial
Angel	Angelic	Comfort	Comfortable
Anger	Angry	Contempt	Contemptuous
Asia	Asiatic	Coward	Cowardly
Angle	Angular	Crime	Criminal
Autumn	Autumnal	Custom	Customary
Beauty	Beautiful	Danger	Dangerous
Black	Blackish	Day	Daily
Blood	Bloody	Earth	Earthly
Body	Bodily		Earthen
Bond	Binding	Ease	Easy
Book	Bookish	Economy	Economical
Boy	Boyish	East	Eastern
Brass	Brazen	Emphasis	Emphatic
Brim	Brimful	Enemy	Inimical
Brother	Brotherly	England	English
Brute	Brutal	Essence	Essential
Burden	Burdensome	Example	Exemplary
Bush	Bushy	Expression	Expressive
Capacity	Capacious	Expense	Expensive
Centre	Central	Face	Facial
Ceremony	Ceremonial	Fable	Fabulous
	Ceremonious	Faith	Faithful
		Fame	Famous
Character	Characteristic	Fate	Fateful
Cheer	Cheerful	Fancy	Fanciful

Nouns	Adjectives	Nouns	Adjectives
Father	Fatherly	Heir	Heredity
Fault	Faulty	Herb	Herbal
Favour	Favourable	Hero	Heroic
Feather	Feathery	Hill	Hilly
Fever	Feverish	Home	Homely
Figure	Figurative	Honour	Honourable
Fire	Fiery	Horn	Horny
Fish	Fishy		Honorary
Flesh	Fleshy	Hour	Hourly
Flower	Flowery	Ice	Icy
Fog	Foggy	Ignorance	Ignorant
Force	Forcible	Industry	Industrial
	Forceful		Industrious
Fool	Foolish	Irony	Ironical
France	French	Jew	Jewish
Friend	Friendly	Joke	Jocular
Frost	Frosty	Joy	Joyful
Fruit	Fruitful		Joyous
Fury	Furious	King	Kingly
Gas	Gaseous	Labour	Laborious
Ghost	Ghostly	Lady	Ladylike
Glory	Glorious	Law	Lawful
Glass	Glassy	Leaf	Leafy
Gloom	Gloomy	Life	Lifelike
God	Godly		Lifeless
Gold	Golden	Limit	Limited
Grass	Grassy		Limitless
Greed	Greedy	Lord	Lordly
Grief	Grievous	Love	Lovely
Hair	Hairy		Loving
Hand	Handy		Lovable
Habit	Habitual	Machine	Mechanical
Harm	Harmful	Man	Manly
	Harmless	Manner	Mannerly
Haste	Hasty	Medicine	Medicinal
Haze	Hazy	Memory	Memorable
Head	Heady	Merchant	Mercantile
Heart	Hearty	Mercy	Merciful
Heaven	Heavenly		Merciless

Nouns	Adjectives	Nouns	Adjectives
Mercury	Mercurial	Price	Precious
Merit	Meritorious	Pride	Proud
Metal	Metallic	Profit	Profitable
Miracle	Miraculous	Prejudice	Prejudicial
Might	Mighty	Question	Questionable
Mirth	Mirthful	Quarrel	Quarrelsome
Milk	Milky	Queen	Queenly
Money	Monetary	Ruin	Ruinous
Month	Monthly	Sand	Sandy
Moment	Momentary	Scholar	Scholarly
Moon	Moony	Science	Scientific
Mother	Motherly	Sedition	Seditious
Muscle	Muscular	Sense	Sensible
Mystery	Mysterious	Service	Serviceable
Nature	Natural	Silk	Silky
Nation	National		Silken
Navy	Naval	Silver	Silvery
Need	Needy	Slave	Slavish
Neighbour	Neighbourly	Smoke	Smoky
Nerve	Nervous	Society	Social
Neuter	Neutral	Solitude	Solitary
Night	Nightly	Spain	Spanish
Notice	Noticeable	Space	Spacious
Number	Numeral	Sponge	Spongy
Ocean	Oceanic	Star	Starry
Office	Official	Store	Story
Oil	Oily	Storm	Stormy
Origin	Original	Sun	Sunny
Ornament	Ornamental	Study	Studious
One	Only	System	Systematic
Palace	Palatial	Sympathy	Sympathetic
Passion	Passionate	Table	Tabular
Peace	Peaceful	Talk	Talkative
People	Popular	Taste	Tasty
Pearl	Pearly		Tasteful
Picture	Picturesque	Terror	Terrible
Play	Playful	Thirst	Thirsty
Population	Populous	Thought	Thoughtful
Practice	Practical		Thoughtless

Nouns	Adjectives	Nouns	Adjectives
Title	Titular	Water	Watery
Tribe	Tribal	Week	Weekly
Trifle	Trifling	Wind	Windy
Trouble	Troublesome	Will	Wilful
Tutor	Tutorial	Winter	Wintry
Type	Typical		Willing
Use	Useful	Woman	Womanly
	Useless	Wood	Womanish
Value	Valuable		Wooden
Vapour	Vapoury	Wool	Woollen
Velvet	Velvety	World	Worldly
Verb	Verbal	Worth	Worthy
Vice	Vicious	Wretch	Wretched
Vigour	Vigorous	Year	Yearly
Virtue	Virtuous	Youth	Youthful
Voice	Vocal	Zeal	Zealous
War	Warlike		

(ii) Formation of Adjectives from Verbs:

Cease	Ceaseless
Move	Moveable
Talk	Talkative
Tire	Tiresome

EXERCISES

1. Form negatives by adding the prefixes or suffixes to the following words.

a)

Theist	Qualify	Efficient
Agree	Accessible	Justice
Approbation	Ability	Abated
Appropriation	Calculable	Certain
Apprehension	Surmountable	Link
Advantage	Compatible	Care
Integrate	Complete	Guilt
Mantle	Credible	Motion
Regard	Disputable	Hope

Help	Law	Fathom
Doubt	Aim	Need
Mercy	Cease	Peer
Faith	Base	Rest

b) Make Verbs from the following words by adding suffixes -ise, -ate, and -fy, making any small changes in spelling that are necessary.

Apology	Domestic	Simple
Active	Familiar	Equal
Symbol	False	Captive
Monopoly	Qualification	Pressure
Civil	Nullity	Immune
Hospital	Commercial	Satire
Clear	Synthetic	Special
Association	Domestic	Sympathy

c) Form Adjectives from the following words by adding -al, -ant, -ate, -ar, -en, -ish, -ive, -ous, -some, and -y, making any small changes in spelling that are necessary.

Fate	Ignore	Accuracy	Friend	Monkey
Nation	Defy	Bound	Boy	Relation
Devotion	Fortune	Wood	Child	Impress
Persuade	Danger	Glory	Treachery	Garrulity

d) The following is a list of Adjectives. Give the Nouns or Verbs with which these Adjectives are associated.

Joyous	Voracious	Distinctive
Capacious	Courageous	Continual
Hideous	Advantageous	Sufficient
Ferocious	Nullity	Ignorant
Fabulous	Falsity	Flamboyant
Angry	Central	Sympathetic
Defensive	Similar	Militant
Obedient	Occasional	Respiratory
Regular	Actual	Factual

2
THE ORDER OF WORDS IN A SENTENCE

We know that a sentence is a combination of words giving a complete sense and it has two parts — a Subject and a Predicate. The Subject refers to the person or thing about which something is said, and the Predicate refers to what is said about the person or thing referred to by the Subject. It can do four kinds of things such as (i) making a statement, (ii) asking a question, (iii) giving a command or making a request, and (iv) making an exclamation. Thus a sentence is called Assertive when it makes a statement or assertion; it is called Interrogative when it asks a question; it is called an Imperative sentence when it gives a command and it is an Exclamatory sentence when it makes an exclamation or expresses strong feeling.

Now it is evident from what has been said above that a sentence cannot be called a sentence if it is merely a group of words without being arranged in the right order. The study of the right arrangement of words in a sentence is of vital importance because the meaning of a sentence depends mainly on the order in which the words composing it are arranged. There may not be anything wrong in the meaning of the words used in a sentence, but the wrong arrangement of the words makes a sentence meaningless. Therefore, adequate attention must be paid to placing the words in a certain order. The rules governing the right arrangement of words in a sentence/sentences are as follows:

1. *The Position of a Subject*

The first thing to be borne in mind is that a sentence has two parts such as a Subject and a Predicate. That is, normally the Subject comes before the Predicate; as,

i) Amalendu is a brilliant boy.
ii) He has lived in Cuttack for many years.
iii) Mr. Roy bought a car.

Here, in example (i) 'Amalendu' is the Subject and 'is a brilliant boy' is the Predicate part of the sentence. Similarly, in example (ii) 'He' is the Subject and 'has lived in Cuttack for many years' is the Predicate part of the sentence. In the third example, 'Mr. Roy' is the Subject and 'bought a car' is the Predicate. These examples show that the Subject precedes the Predicate part of the sentence. Further, these examples indicate that the Subject is placed before the Verb. Thus, as a rule, the Subject comes before the Predicate part and the Verb of the sentence.

2. *The Position and Order of Objects*

a) The Object normally comes after the Verb in a sentence; as,
The police punished *the thief.*
Kamal is writing *letters.*
Shovan has bought a *wristwatch.*
We eat *rice.*

b) In a sentence, if the Verb governs two Objects, one Direct and the other Indirect, then the Indirect Object normally comes before the Direct Object; as,
I gave *HIM* (Indirect) a *PEN* (Direct).
The bookseller sent *HIM* (Indirect) the *BOOKS* (Direct) by post.
Give your *FATHER* (Indirect) my *KIND REGARDS* (Direct).
Sometimes this order can be reversed if

i) the Indirect Object is much longer than the Direct,
ii) the Indirect Object is used for the sake of emphasis; as,
I gave the pen *to anyone who asked for it.*
The bookseller sent the books *to anyone who placed orders for them.*
Give the pen *to the poor boy,* not *to him.*
Send the money *to Ramesh,* or *anyone else you like.*

c) Such verbs as explain, describe, announce, confide, entrust, introduce, suggest, propose, say, etc., have two Objects and in these cases the Indirect Object must be used after the Direct; as,

i) The Principal introduced the Chief Guest *to the members of his staff.*

ii)   He described his symptoms in great detail *to the family doctor.*

iii) No one really likes to confide a secret *to a complete stranger.*

iv)   The Director of Health proposed a Child Welfare Scheme *to the Government.*

v)   He described his physical features in detail *to me.*

vi)   He suggested this idea *to me.*

vii) The teacher announced the rules of the examination *to the students.*

viii) He will entrust this responsibility *to his friend.*

3.   *The Provisional or Introductory Subjects — 'It' and 'There'*

a)   When a sentence is introduced by 'it' as a provisional Subject, the real Subject comes after the Verb. The real Subject which is replaced by 'it', is usually an infinitive construction or a Noun Clause; as,

i)   It is a matter of pride *to win the game* = *To win the game* is a matter of pride.

ii)   It is good *to be here* = *To be here* is good.

iii) It was necessary *to work hard* = *To work hard* was necessary.

iv)   It was nice *to see her again* = *To see her again* was nice.

v)   It is a pity *that he is deaf* = *That he is deaf* is a pity.

vi)   It is true *that he cheated* = *That he cheated* is true.

vii) *What you say* is not the fact = It is not the fact *what you say.*

viii) It has been found impossible *to reach the top of the mountain* =*To reach the top of the mountain* has been found impossible.

ix)   *What they discussed in the meeting* is not known = It is not known *what they discussed in the meeting.*

x)   *That he has been most unwise* is clear = It is clear *that he has been most unwise.*

b)   The provisional Subject 'it' is used for the sake of emphasis.

Look at the following sentences:

i)   *Manoj* met the new Chairman.
It was *Manoj* who met the new Chairman.
Manoj met *the new Chairman.*
It was the new Chairman that Manoj met.

ii)   *Yesterday evening* Manoj met the new Chairman in the Conference Hall.

It was yesterday evening that Manoj met the new Chairman in the Conference Hall.

Manoj met the new Chairman *in the Conference Hall.*

It was in the Conference Hall, that Manoj met the new Chairman.

These examples show that we can give emphasis to any part of the sentence by putting it at the beginning after the words 'it is (was)'. The rest of the sentence then follows as a Clause. If the emphasised part or a word of a sentence is the Subject and a person, the Clause must begin with 'who'; as,

It was Manoj who met the new Chairman.

But if 'it' refers to the Object, 'that' is used or omitted to form the contact Clause and in all other cases that may be used; as,

It was the new Chairman (that) Manoj met.

It was in the Conference Hall (that) Manoj met him.

It was yesterday evening (that) Manoj met him.

'That' is not normally used in ordinary conversation, when it is not used as the Subject of a Verb.

c)   The provisional Subject 'it' in questions.

The examples, given in (b) may be also used in question forms. Generally, the word (that) is omitted in question forms. The following sentences in which the provisional Subject 'it' is used, are changed into questions:

   i) It was the Chairman I met yesterday.
      Who was it you met yesterday?
  ii) It was at the foot of the hill that he saw a peacock.
      Where was it he saw a peacock?
 iii) It was half an hour ago I saw them last.
      When was it you saw them last?
  iv) It was because he is so young that he cannot understand.
      Why is it he cannot understand?
   v) It was three years ago that he passed his final examinations.
      How long was it since he passed his final examination?
  vi) It was the one on the right that fell and got broken.
      Which was it that fell and got broken?

   d)   When a sentence is introduced by 'there', the Subject
        normally comes after the Verb; as,
   i) There was a book on the table.
  ii) There is someone at the door.

iii) There can be no doubt about it.
iv) There is no stopping him.
v) There has been a rise in prices.
vi) There will be a meeting in the staff common room of the college tomorrow.

4. *The Position of the Complement*
   In a sentence, the Complement usually comes after the verb. The following examples indicate the use of Complements:

   i) Amarendra became *a doctor.*
   ii) My friend looks *very sad.*
   iii) You are an *honest man.*
   iv) He is *a learned man.*
   v) He seems *to be very unhappy.*
   vi) He appears *to be very learned.*
   vii) The students elected him *president.*
   viii) The Government of Orissa declared Ravenshaw College, Cuttack, *autonomous.*
   ix) The Government made him an *Honorary Secretary.*
   x) The king made him a *knight.*

5. *Inversion of the Subject and Verb after certain Adverbs*
   There are certain Adverbs which are either restrictive or negative in their meaning. They are as follows:

   Scarcely, hardly, rarely, never, little, neither, nor, even, less, seldom, at no time, by no means, nowhere, etc.

   Besides these Adverbs, there are also certain other restrictive Adverbs used with 'only'. The following are such Adverbs:

   Only by chance, only then, only today, only yesterday, only with difficulty, only on rare occasions, only by luck.

   When any of these Adverbs is placed at the beginning of the sentence, the Subject usually follows the Verbs, as in a question; as,

   Hardly had we got into the country when it began to rain.
   Hardly had I reached the station when the train left for Calcutta.
   Never have I heard such nonsense in all my life.
   Seldom does she go out.
   Rarely does he come here after tea.

   When the simple present or past is used in the sentence, the auxiliary Verb 'do' can be used as in a question; as,

   Nowhere did he get better facilities for his education than in Delhi.

Little does he know that the police are about to arrest him.
Little does he know how stupid he is.

These Adverbs, however, can be placed in positions where they do not affect the order of the Verb and its Subject in the sentences as in the Rule No. 6 that follows.

6.   *The Position and Order of Adverbs*

a)   There are many Adverbs and Adverbial expressions of more than one word which follow the Verb and the Object, if there is one; as,
     He finished his work *very soon.*
     He read the book *carefully.*
     She loves music *very much.*

b)   The Adverb of Manner expressed in a single word can normally be placed between the Subject and the Verb when we want to emphasise how an action is performed; as,
     He *rarely* comes here.
     He *seldom* speaks well.
     She *beautifully* sang the song.
     He *quickly* closed the windows.

7.   *Position of Pre-verb Adverbs in Sentences*

There are certain common Adverbs which are normally placed before the Verbs, with different tenses. Such Adverbs are 'still', 'just', 'already', 'yet'. The Adverbs of Frequency such as 'seldom', 'always', 'often', 'rarely', 'sometimes', 'generally', 'frequently', 'usually', 'never', 'occasionally', and the restrictive adverbs such as 'partly', 'largely', 'in no way', 'wholly', 'scarcely', 'hardly', 'by no means', 'only', 'little', are used with Anomalous Verbs in short answers, with different tenses and with the Verb 'to be'. Examples are as follows:

a)   With different tenses:
     We *often go* there.
     We *have often been* there.
     He *has never gone* there.
     He *will rarely go* there.
     He *would sometimes go* there.
     He *frequently goes* there.
     He *occasionally goes* to the cinema.
     He *generally talks* about his own life.
     He *usually avoids* him.

b)   With anomalous verbs:
      He *can sometimes go* there.
      He *can usually read* twelve hours a day.
      He *must occasionally pay* his visit to your house.
      He *must hardly go* there.
      He *must scarcely go* there.
      He *must always read* twelve hours a day.
      He *can only come* to your help.

c)   In short answers :
      They *usually* have.
      We *only* can.
      He *often* has.

d)   With the Verb 'to be':
      You *are always* lazy.
      He *is generally* happy.
      The train *is never* late.
      He *has always been* ill.
      He *is partially* to blame for the disaster.
      They *were largely responsible* for the accident.
      It *is by no means* certain that you will succeed.

But when there are several Adverbs in a sentence, the usual order in which they follow the Verb is first, the adverb of Manner; second, the Adverb of Place; and third, the Adverb of Time; as,

He has been working *hard* (manner) in the *field* (place) all *day* (time).

He taught grammar *satisfactorily* (manner) in the *classroom* (place) *yesterday* (time).

There are certain variations in the order. (i) When there is a Verb of Movement, the Adverb of Place can be put immediately after the Verb to complete the sense, and (ii) in case of a long sentence with other Adverb in it, the Adverb of Time must be placed at the beginning of the sentence; as,

i)   He *walked* (movement) to the *conference hall* (place) in a hurry last night.
      He *flew* (movement) to *Japan* (place) by air last summer.
      The plane *arrived* (movement) at the *airport* (place) early.

ii)   *Yesterday* (time) he unexpectedly left for Delhi by the evening train.
      At eleven o'clock (time) they returned with their friends to their hotel.

Yesterday (time) he regretfully said goodbye at the station.
After (time) dinner he quietly spoke to him in the hall.

8. *When there are several Adverbs of*

a) The same type in a sentence, the more exact can be placed before the more general.

b) When there are two Adverbs of Manner, first the shorter must be joined with the longer by 'and'. The examples of these two rules are as follows:

i) He arrived at six o'clock this morning.
They are leaving in the afternoon for Italy on Thursday next week.

ii) Hand it carefully to me with your right hand.
Read this book carefully and seriously.
Recommend his case strongly and impartially.
Punish him severely and mercilessly.
Deal with the problem strongly and tactfully.
But Adverbs of Manner are normally used immediately before the Past Participle in a passive sentence; as,
It has been *carelessly* thrown away.
He has been *completely* restored to health.
He is respected *highly* by his colleagues.
The roof has been *seriously* damaged.

9. *Position and Order of Adjectives*

a) An Adjective may normally go before the word it describes. In other words (i) it may be placed close to the Noun it qualifies or (ii) it may be used as part of the Predicate of the sentence. The following sentences illustrate the use of Adjectives before the Noun:

i) A *black* cat caught a *white* mouse.
The *old* servant thanked his *kind* master.
A *new* idea dawned upon his mind.
Sometimes, however, the Adjective may come after the Noun, especially when it is combined with a phrase, or when more than one Adjective is used.
This film, *popular* with the masses, has hardly any merits.
A beggar, *old, weak and blind,* stood at the gate.

ii) The following sentences illustrate the use of an Adjective as part of the Predicate.
The poor old beggar was very *grateful*.
The students in the college seemed very *happy*.

b) An Adjective Phrase comes directly after its Noun; as,
The roof of the house *fell in.*
Your father was a man *of high character.*
He is a man *of extraordinary calibre.*

c) When two or more Adjectives are used to describe a word, we usually place the one with the most general or subjective meaning first and the most specific and objective last; as,
The old, useless clothes; An incredible, fantastic ghost story; A poor defenceless girl; A fine old Tudor farm-house.

d) When two equally exact Adjectives are used, the shorter must be placed first; as,
A long, boring, technical lecture; A happy, active, intelligent boy; A rich indigestible food; A quiet well-ordered household; An attractive broad-brimmed Mexican hat.

(e) Sometimes for the sake of emphasis, two Adjectives are joined by 'and'; as,
A new and useful idea; A fine and faithful man; A kind and honest man; A dark and stormy night; A beautiful and interesting story.

10. *The Position of 'Both' and 'All'*
The words 'both' and 'all' which have two alternative positions in a sentence can be used (i) with compound tenses, (ii) with simple tenses, and (iii) with the Verb 'to be'. They are used as follows:

i) 'Both' used with compound tenses.
Both his friends have done their work.
His friends have *both* done their work.
Both our sisters have prepared for their examinations.
Our sisters have *both* prepared for their examinations.
Both his servants have accepted their respective assignments.
His servants have *both* accepted their respective assignments.

ii) 'All' used with simple tenses.
All the lights in the town went out suddenly.
The lights *all* went out in the town suddenly.
All the books from the shelves fell in suddenly.

The books *all* fell in from the shelves suddenly.
All the family enjoyed the picnic.
The family *all* enjoyed the picnic.

iii) 'All' used with the Verb 'to be'.
All his brothers are old.
His brothers are *all* old.
All his friends are happy.
His friends are *all* happy.

11.   *The Order of Words in Indirect Questions*

The Indirect Question which is grammatically not a question at all, does not have an inversion of the Verb and Subject like the Direct Question. Normally the Auxiliary Verb 'do' is used in a Direct Question. But there is no inversion in an Indirect Question and as such the use of the Auxiliary Verb 'do' is not necessary. The following are the examples:

Direct Question :   'Where are you going?'
Indirect   :   I should like to know where you are going.
Direct   :   'What do you mean?'
Indirect   :   Tell me what you mean.
Direct   :   'How much do you love her?'
Indirect   :   Tell me how much you love her.
Direct   :   'Can he help her?'
Indirect   :   She wants to ask him whether he can help her.
Direct   :   'Why have you disobeyed my orders?'
Indirect   :   Tell me why you have disobeyed my orders.
Direct   :   'When do they intend to leave?'
Indirect   :   They have not told me when they intend to leave.

EXERCISES

1.   Arrange the words in the following sentences in the usual order:
   i)   Playing hobby is football his.
   ii) Mistakes made many while he sums the out working.
   iii) What he has done with the money?
   iv) His satisfaction exploited to he opportunity this.
   v)   When you did see him last?
   vi) That work done they people are the who have.

vii) Your friend is away probably.

viii) What he has done for you?

ix) Now raining it is.

x) There many workers in that are factory.

2. The following sentences are examples of Inversion. Rewrite them by arranging the words in their usual order:

a) A moment now he slacked his speed.

b) Blame me you cannot.

c) Him they blame the most.

d) Blessed are the meek and the innocent.

e) Sign this bond he shall.

f) Seldom do they go out in the evenings these days.

g) Never in all his life he has seen such a beautiful sight as this.

h) Hardly had he finished when somebody knocked at the door.

i) Nowhere did you make a greater impression than in Bangalore.

j) Never have I heard such silly things.

3. Write the Adjectives supplied in the correct place after the words they describe in the following sentences:

i) Ramesh inherited a mansion (ruined past repair).

ii) His house was for sale (empty and deserted).

iii) The breeze revived them (fresh from the recent rain).

iv) Hrishikesh received a letter (written in red ink).

v) The cupboard is mine (standing against that wall).

vi) His speech came to an end at last (dull and uninteresting).

vii) A garden lay before us (filled with flowers).

viii) The labourers of the factory went on a strike (dissatisfied with their wages).

ix) The mob began to disperse (drunk and disorderly).

x) The drawing-room attracted their attention (furnished in the latest style).

4. Put the Adverbs given in brackets in the correct place before the Verb in the following sentences:

i) They come to see him on Sunday. (sometimes)

ii) You can understand their problems. (to some extent)

iii) His brother is responsible for the loss he suffered in his business. (largely)

iv) Hiren would have been a great support to his family, had he not settled in America. (always)

v) She was responsible for the ruin of his life. (completely)

vi) You have seen a village fair. (never)

vii) He will do that work. (rarely)

viii) They had come in when the telephone rang. (only just)

ix) They understand the problems you have. (little)

x) His friend has told him a thousand times not to do it. (already)

3
COMPOUND WORDS

There are many compound words in English and they are also used frequently in our conversation and writing. A compound word is usually composed of two or more parts which are themselves words. The learner must know the meaning of the compound words before he makes use of them in his writing. The following is a list of compound words:

A) About-turn : in the opposite direction.

About-face : turn and face the opposite way.

Above-board : without any deception or concealment.

Above-mentioned : mentioned above or in the same page.

Above-named : name given above.

Age-long : going on for a long time.

Air-bed : mattress inflated with air.

Air-bladder : bladder filled with air.

Air-conditioned : supplied with air that is purified and kept at a certain temperature and degree.

Air-cooled : cooled by a current of air.

Aircraft : aeroplanes, airships.

Air-crew : crew of an aircraft.

Air-cushion : cushion inflated with air.

Air-drop : dropping by parachutes from aircraft.

Airfield : area of open, level ground with buildings, offices, etc., for operations of aircraft.

Airframe : complete structure of an aircraft.

Airgraph	:	system of micro-filming and sending letters in this way.
Airgun	:	gun in which compressed air is used to propel the charge.
Airhostess	:	stewardess in an airliner.
Airlift	:	large-scale transport of persons or supplies by air.
Airliner	:	passenger-carrying aircraft for public service.
Air-lock	:	compartment with airtight doors at each end.
Airmail	:	mail carried by air.
Air-minded	:	looking upon flying as a normal and necessary method of transport.
Air-pocket	:	atmospheric condition causing an aircraft to drop some distance.
Airport	:	public flying ground for commercial use by airliners.
Air-shaft	:	passage for air into a mine.
Airing-cupboard	:	warmed cupboard in which to keep bedsheets, towels, etc.
Airtight	:	so tight as not to admit air.
Almshouse	:	house founded by charity.
Altarpiece	:	painting or sculpture placed above and behind an altar.
Anglo-French	:	between Great Britain and France.
Anglo-Catholic	:	(member) of the party in the Anglican Church that insists upon its unbroken connection with the early Christian Church and that objects to being called Protestant.
Anglo-Saxon	:	of English descent; one of the races of people who settled in England from North-west Europe before the Norman conquest.
Ant-eater	:	name of an animal that lives on ants.
Ant-hill	:	mound of earth built by ants, or pile of earth.
Anti-Semite	:	person prejudiced against Jews.
Arrow-head	:	pointed end of an arrow.

Ash-pan	:	tray into which ashes drop from a fire.
Ash-tray	:	small saucer for tobacco ash.
Attache-case	:	small, flat, rectangular box for documents.
Awe-inspiring	:	filling with awe or fear.
Awe-stricken or	:	struck with awe.
Awe-struck	:	
Back-bencher	:	person occupying a seat not in the front bench.
Back-bite	:	speak evil of a person in his absence.
Back-blocks	:	land that is a long way from a railway, river or the sea coast and is sparsely populated.
Backbone	:	line of bones down the middle of the back; chief support.
Backcloth	:	painted cloth hung at the back of the stage in a theatre.
Backdate	:	date back to a time in the past.
Backdoor	:	door at the back of a building; secret or underhand means.
Backdown	:	withdrawal from one's position or claims.
Back-formation	:	process of making a word that appears to be the root of a longer word.
Background	:	that part of a view or scene that serves as a setting for the chief objects; contemporary condition; person's past experiences, etc.
Back-space	:	press the special key that sends the roller and paper to the right instead of to the left.
Backstage	:	behind the scenes.
Backstairs	:	staircase from servant's quarters.
Backstays	:	set of ropes from the masthead to the sides of a ship.
Boatman	:	a man who has charge of a boat.
Bystander	:	a person who stands near, an onlooker.
Cabin-boy	:	boy who waits on officers and passengers.

Cabin-class	:	Class between first and tourist class.
Cable-car	:	a car for passengers going up a steep hillside, worked by a cable.
Cable-railway	:	a stationary engine, funicular railway.
Carefree	:	free from care
Careworn	:	troubled by anxiety.
Carrier-pigeon	:	pigeon used to carry messages because it can find its way home from a distant place.
Catwalk	:	narrow footway along a bridge or through a mass of machinery.
Chicken-hearted	:	timid, cowardly.
Cross-examine	:	to question a person on all sides of a subject.
Deaf-mute	:	one who is both deaf and dumb.
Down-train	:	a train proceeding from the principal terminus of a railway.
Double-dealing	:	a dealing in which no sincerity is to be found.
Foster-child	:	a child nursed or brought up by one who is not his or her parent.
Freehold	:	a property held free of duty or rent.
Go-between	:	a person who is an agent between two parties.
Godsend	:	an unexpected piece of good fortune.
Greenhouse	:	a house which shelters tender plants from the cold weather.
Greenroom	:	the retiring room of actors in a theatre.
Henpecked	:	a man who is completely under the control of his wife.
Holiday	:	a day given not to labour but to amusement.
Hush-money	:	money given as a bribe to hush or make one keep silent.
Jailbird	:	an offender who has often been in jail for his crimes.
Keepsake	:	something that is given to one to be kept for the sake of the giver.

Marksman	:	a man who can hit the mark.
Namesake	:	one who bears the same name as another.
Outlaw	:	a person who is deprived of the protection of the law.
Pickpocket	:	a person who steals from other people's pockets.
Passport	:	a written warrant granting permission to travel in a foreign country.
Pitfall	:	a pit dug for wild beasts to fall into.
Ringleader	:	the leader in the ring of a dance; leader in a riot or gang.
Scarecrow	:	anything, usually an effigy, set up to scare away crows or other birds.
Scapegoat	:	one who is made to suffer for the misdeeds of another.
Seasick	:	sick because of the rolling of a vessel at sea.
Shoeblack	:	one who blacks and cleans shoes.
Shop-lifter	:	one who steals anything from a shop.
Short-hand	:	an art by which writing is made shorter and easier.
Spokesman	:	one who speaks for others.
Sportsman	:	a man devoted to sports.
Stronghold	:	a place strong enough to hold out against attack.
Swordsman	:	a man skilled in the use of swords.
Telltale	:	one who officiously tells others about the private concerns or misdeeds of people.
Tempest-tossed	:	beaten or swept by a tempest.
Terror-struck or Terror-stricken	:	struck with terror.
Thorough-going	:	complete.
Thorough-paced	:	uncompromising.
Thoroughfare	:	road or street, especially one much used by the traffic and open at both ends.

Threshing-floor	:	part on which grain is threshed out.
Thunderstorm	:	storm of thunder and lightning, usually with heavy rain.
Thunder-struck	:	amazed.
Time-limit	:	limited period of time.
Time-saving	:	serving to save time.
Time-server	:	one who acts not according to principles, but according to self-interest, especially one who is always trying to please powerful people.
Turncoat	:	one who turns his coat, i.e. abandons his principles or party.
Typewriter	:	machine with which one prints letters on paper using the fingers on a keyboard.
Two-fold	:	double.
Two-handed	:	needing two hands to use.
Up-train	:	train proceeding towards the principal terminus of a railway.
Upstart	:	one who has suddenly started up. i.e., risen from low life to wealth, etc.
Waylay	:	to lie in the way for a person to stop a person on the way for an evil purpose.
Well-read (person)	:	a person who has read many good authors.
Whitewash	:	To wash with a liquid to whiten walls.
Woodman or Woodsman	:	one who fells trees.
Wooden-headed	:	stupid, stiff, clumsy.
Wood-craft	:	knowledge of forest conditions; skill in finding one's way in woods and forests, especially as used in hunting.
Wool-gathering	:	absent-mindedness.
Word-book	:	vocabulary, list of words with meanings.
Word-painter	:	person who can describe vividly in words.

Word-perfect	:	knowing, able to repeat, a poem, a part in a play, etc., by heart.
Word-picture	:	vivid description in words.
Word-splitting	:	sophistry, making of distinctions in meaning.
Work-bench	:	table at which a mechanic does his work.
Workbook	:	book with outlines of a subject of study.
Work-day	:	day for work.
Work-house	:	public institution for homeless people in a parish.
Workman	:	man who earns a living by physical labour or at machines, etc.
Workmanlike	:	characteristic of a good workman.
Workmanship	:	quality as seen in something made.
Workshop	:	room or building in which things are made or repaired.
Work-shy	:	disinclined to work.
Work-study	:	study of housework which may be done efficiently and economically.
Work-table	:	table with drawers for sewing materials, etc.
Worldwide	:	found in or spread over all parts of the world.
Yule-log	:	log of wood burnt on Christmas Eve.
Zero-hour	:	time at which operations are to begin.

B) (i) The following compounds can be expanded into equivalent phrases by using appropriate Prepositions to connect the words which they are formed of.

Blood-stained	:	stained *with* blood.
Fire-engine	:	engine *for* fire.
Fire-proof	:	proof *against* fire.
Fire-bomb	:	bomb burning fiercely *for* causing destruction.
Fire-brand	:	a person aiming *at* social or political strife.
Fire-brick	:	proof *against* fire.
Fire-clay	:	clay used *for* fire-bricks.

Compound Words

Fire-house	:	hose-pipe used *for* extinguishing fire.
Fire-plug	:	connection *for* a fire-hose.
Firewood	:	wood prepared *for* lighting fires.
Hard-hearted	:	hard *at* heart.
Heartsick	:	sick *at* heart.
Homesick	:	longing *for* home, sick for home.
Home-bound	:	bound *for* home.
Horse-dealers	:	dealers *in* horses.
Star-gazers	:	gazers *at* stars.
Self-confidence	:	confidence *in* one's own self.
Soft-hearted	:	soft *at* heart.
Teacup	:	cup *for* tea.
Thumb-impression	:	impression or sign made *by* thumb.
Time-bound	:	bound *by* time.
Time-tested	:	tested *by time.*
Time-honoured	:	proved or honoured *by* time.
Weather-bound	:	bound *by* weather.

ii) The following pairs of words indicate the compounds formed from them:

Brass and face	:	brazen-faced (shameless).
Finger and light	:	light-fingered (thievish).
Fist and close	:	close-fisted (niggardly).
Grain and cross	:	cross-grained (perverse).
Head and hard	:	hard-headed (shrewd, intelligent).
Skin and thick	:	thick-skinned (stolid).
Skin and thin	:	thin-skinned (irritable).

iii) The following words can be used adjectively to form Compound Nouns:
Air, court, cart, earth, gate, head, house, lamp, life, lump, office, race, water, wood.

Air	:	air-pump
Cart	:	cart-horse
Court	:	courtyard
Earth	:	earthwork
Gate	:	gateman
Head	:	headache
House	:	house-rent
Lamp	:	lamp-oil
Lump	:	lump-sugar

	:	lifeboat
	:	office-bearer
	:	race-horse
	:	woodblock
	:	water-bag

iv) The following words are used adverbially to form Compound Adjectives:

Coal, foot, head, ice, knee, moon, sea, stone, snow, sky, storm, skin, sun, weather.

Coal	:	coal-black
Foot	:	footsore
Head	:	headstrong
Ice	:	ice-cold
Knee	:	knee-deep
Moon	:	moonstruck
Sea	:	sea-green
Skin	:	skin-deep
Sky	:	sky-blue
Snow	:	snow-white
Stone	:	stone-blind
Storm	:	storm-bound
Sun	:	sunburnt
Weather	:	weather-bound

v) The following words are used as Adverbs to form Compound Adjectives:

Dog, far, hen, post, purse, red, thick, time, top, water, world, year.

Dog	:	dog-weary
Far	:	far-fetched
Hen	:	henpecked
Post	:	post-free
Purse	:	purse-proud
Red	:	red-hot
Thick	:	thick-headed
Time	:	time-tutored
Top	:	top-heavy
Water	:	Water-proof
World	:	worldwide
Year	:	year-old

vi) The following words can be used as Adjectives to form Compound Nouns:

Arm, beauty, blue, case, check, cloud, cock, cork, crown, cut, ice, noble, quick, sweet.

Arm	:	arm-chair
Beauty	:	beauty-sleep
Blue	:	blue-bell
Case	:	case-bottle
Check	:	check-clerk
Cloud	:	cloud-burst
Cork	:	cork-screw
Cock	:	cock-fight
Crown	:	crown prince
Cut	:	cut-throat
Ice	:	ice-cream
Noble	:	nobleman
Quick	:	quicksand
Sweet	:	sweetheart

C) Diminutives:

- aster : poet*aster*, ole*aster*, dis*aster*.

- el, -le : dams*el*, cast*le*, mod*el*, citad*el*, mors*el*, parc*el*, satch*el* (sack)

- icle, -cule : arti*cle*, parti*cle*, animal*cule*, curri*cle*, cuti*cle*, corpus*cle*, pinna*cle*.

- ule : glob*ule*, pill*ule*, nod*ule*.

- et, -let : lock*et*, lanc*et*, pock*et*, pack*et*, brace*let*, stream*let*, brook*let*, leaf*let*, rivu*let*, ring*let*, root*let*, arm*let*, ank*let*, bill*et*, eye*let*, ham*let* (from 'home')

- ot : fagg*ot*, chari*ot*, parr*ot*, magg*ot*, ball*ot*, piv*ot*.

- ette : etiqu*ette*, statu*ette*, cigar*ette*, waggon*ette*.

EXERCISES

1. Convert the following compound words into equivalent phrases using appropriate Prepositions:

Bare-footed, blood-stained, colour-blind, fire-proof, hard-hearted, heartsick, homesick, lame-footed, self-confidence, weather-bound.

2. Form Compound Nouns with the following words used Adjectively:
    a) Court, office, common, gate, lump, race, snow, ice, knee, sea, water, lamp.
    b) Form Compound Adjectives with the following words used as Adverbs:
        Far, red, time, world, top, thick, post, dog, water, hen.

3. Explain the following compounds:
    Age-long, air-crew, air-pocket, airtight, air-lock, fire-arms, backstays, carrier-pigeon, hush-money, godsend, double-dealing, pitfall, tempest-tossed, thoroughfare, wood-craft, word-painter, workmanship, yule-log, zero-hour.

4
SINGLE WORDS FOR GROUPS OF WORDS

There are certain things, ideas or beliefs which can be expressed in single words. Sometimes the learner uses a group of words to express them, the reason for this being a lack of command over such words. When a single word conveys the meanings of so many words there is no need to use a group of words. Therefore, adequate attention must be given to such single words so that one may use them in one's conversation or writing. The following is a list of single words for groups of words:

Single words	:	Groups of words
Abrogate	:	To do away with a rule.
Accelerate	:	To increase the speed.
Advocate	:	Person who pleads in a court of justice.
Aggravate	:	To increase the gravity of an offence or intensity of a dispute.
Alien	:	One who resides in a country of which he is not a citizen.
Alimony	:	Allowance due to a wife from her husband on separation.
Amateur	:	One who plays a game for pleasure and not professionally
Ambassador	:	A minister representing a sovereign or state in a foreign country.
Amnesty	:	A general pardon of political offenders.
Amphibian	:	Animals equally at home on land or at sea.
Anarchy	:	The absence of government in a country, disorder.

Animate	:	Objects possessed of life.
Annihilate	:	To completely destroy or blot out.
Anniversary	:	Yearly return of the date of an event or celebration of this.
Annuity	:	Fixed sum of money paid to somebody yearly as income during his life-time.
Anomaly	:	Deviation from the common rule or standard.
Anonymous	:	Of unknown or unadmitted authorship.
Answerable	:	Liable to be called to account.
Anthology	:	Collection of poems or pieces of prose or of both.
Anthropology	:	Science of man especially of the beginnings, development, customs and beliefs of mankind.
Antibiotic	:	A substance capable of destroying or preventing the growth of bacteria.
Antic	:	Grotesque movement intended to amuse.
Antidote	:	A medicine to counteract the effect of poison.
Antiquarian	:	Connected with the study of customs and events of ancient times.
Antiseptic	:	Anything that counteracts putrefaction or decay.
Antonym	:	A word opposite in meaning.
Aphonia	:	Total loss of voice.
Apostate	:	One who abandons his religious faith.
Aquarium	:	A tank for fishes or water plants.
Aquatic	:	Living in or upon water.
Armistice	:	The cessation of warfare before a treaty is signed.
Ascetic	:	A person who starves his body for the good of the soul.
Atheist	:	One who does not believe in the existence of God.
Atmosphere	:	The mass of air surrounding the earth.
Attenuate	:	To make thin or fine or to reduce the strength.
Audience	:	An assembly of listeners.
Autobiography	:	The life-history of a person written by himself.

Autocracy	:	An absolute government.
Aviary	:	A place where birds are kept.
Bathroom	:	A place for washing.
Bibliophile	:	A great lover or collector of books.
Bigamy	:	The state of having two wives or husbands at the same time.
Biography	:	The life-history of a person written by another.
Blasphemy	:	The act of talking impiously about sacred things.
Blonde	:	A man or woman with skin and hair of vellow or auburn colour.
Botany	:	Science of the life of plants.
Brittle	:	Liable to be easily broken.
Bureaucracy	:	Government by officials.
Cannibal	:	One who eats human flesh.
Carnivore	:	Eater of flesh.
Cemetery	:	A place for burial of dead bodies.
Colleagues	:	Persons who work in the same department of an office.
Conductor	:	A person who collects fares on a public vehicle.
Congenital	:	Belonging or pertaining to an individual from birth.
Congregation	:	An assembly of worshippers.
Conscription	:	Compulsory enlistment for military or other services.
Contemporary	:	A person who lives at the same time as another.
Cosmopolitan	:	A person who is familiar with many different countries, belonging to all parts of the world.
Credulous	:	A person who easily believes what is told to him.
Crew	:	Workers and servants on a boat.
Democracy	:	Government by the representatives of the people.
Dictatorship	:	Government carried on by an absolute ruler.
Dispensary	:	A place fitted up for making medicines.

Dramatist	:	One who writes a drama.
Draw	:	The result of a match in which neither party wins.
Effeminate	:	One whose manners are more like those of a woman than those of a man.
Emigrant	:	One who leaves his own country to settle elsewhere.
Emissary	:	A person sent on a mission.
Eternal	:	Having no beginning or end to its existence, existing for ever.
Extempore	:	A speech made without preparation.
Factotum	:	Male servant employed to do all kinds of work.
Fastidious	:	Hard to please.
Fatal or mortal	:	Resulting in death.
Fatalist	:	One who believes in fate.
Florist	:	A person who sells flowers.
Forgery	:	Signature of someon else's name without his permission, or other counterfeiting of a document.
Germicide	:	A substance that kills germs.
Goldsmith	:	One who makes ornaments in gold.
Gullible	:	Person who is easily deceived.
Homicide	:	The killer or killing of a human being.
Honorary	:	Conferred as an honour, or performed without pay.
Hospitable	:	Fond of entertaining guests.
Illegal	:	Contrary to law.
Illegible	:	Incapable of being read.
Illicit	:	Forbidden, prohibited by law.
Illiterate	:	A person who can neither read nor write.
Immigrant	:	One who comes as a settler into a foreign country.
Impenetrable	:	Incapable of being penetrated.
Imperceptible	:	Incapable of being perceived by the senses.
Impracticable	:	Incapable of being put into practice.
Impregnable	:	Incapable of being taken by force of arms.
Inaccessible	:	Incapable of being accessible.
Inadmissible	:	Incapable of being admitted.
Inaudible	:	Incapable of being heard.

Incombustible	:	Incapable of being burnt.
Incredible	:	Incapable of being believed.
Indefensible	:	Incapable of being defended.
Indestructible	:	Incapable of being destroyed.
Indispensable	:	Incapable of being dispensed with.
Indivisible	:	Incapable of being divided.
Ineligible	:	One who is not able to be elected or selected under the rules.
Inevitable	:	Incapable of being avoided.
Inexcusable	:	Incapable of being justified or excused.
Inexhaustible	:	Incapable of being tired out.
Inexplicable	:	Incapable of being explained or accounted for.
Inexplicit	:	Not definitely or clearly expressed.
Inexpressible	:	Incapable of being expressed in words.
Infallible	:	Not being able to make a mistake.
Infanticide	:	The murder of a newborn infant.
Inflammable	:	Capable of being easily set on fire.
Insecticide	:	A substance that kills insects.
Insoluble	:	Incapable of being solved.
Insolvent or Bankrupt	:	One who is not able to pay one's debt.
Insurmountable	:	Incapable of being overcome.
Invincible	:	Incapable of being conquered.
Inviolable	:	Not to be disturbed, disobeyed or treated disrespectfully.
Invisible	:	That cannot be seen.
Invulnerable	:	Incapable of being wounded.
Irreconciliable	:	Incapable of being reconciled.
Irrecoverable	:	Incapable of being recovered or regained.
Irreparable	:	Incapable of being repaired.
Irrevocable	:	Incapable of being altered or recalled.
Kitchen	:	Room where food is cooked.
Laboratory	:	A place fitted up for scientific experiments.
Laundry	:	A place where clothes are cleaned.
Laxative	:	A medicine tending to loosen the bowels.
Linguist	:	One who knows many languages.
Logic	:	The science of reasoning.
Mammals	:	Animals which suckle their young.
Manuscript	:	A paper written by hand.

Martyr	:	One who undergoes the penalty of death for persistence in one's faith.
Matricide	:	The murder of one's own mother.
Mercenary	:	Working only for money or other reward or inspired by love of money.
Mesalliance	:	Marriage with a person of lower social position.
Mesmerism	:	Control over somebody's personality and actions by the exercise of willpower.
Messiah	:	Person expected by the Jews to come and set them free.
Metamorphosis	:	Change of form or character by natural growth or development.
Microphone	:	Instrument for changing sound waves into electrical waves as in telephones, radio, etc.
Microscope	:	Instrument with lenses for making very small, and near objects appear larger.
Misanthrope Misanthropist	:	One who hates mankind.
Mortal	:	Subject to death.
Navigator	:	One who is qualified to navigate
Notorious	:	One who has an evil reputation.
Novelist	:	One who writes a novel.
Nursery	:	A place where young plants are reared.
Obsolete	:	That which is no longer used or that is out of date.
Octogenarian	:	A person whose age is from 80 to 89 years.
Odalisque	:	Eastern female slave or concubine in a seraglio in older times.
Offing	:	A part of the sea distant from the point of observation but visible.
Omnipotent	:	Being all-powerful.
Omnipresent	:	Being present everywhere.
Omniscient	:	Knowing everything, having infinite knowledge.
Omnivorous	:	Eating all kinds of food.
Opaque	:	Not allowing the passage of light.
Optician	:	One who sells spectacles.
Optimist	:	One who looks at the bright side of things.
Orator	:	One who makes an eloquent public speech.

Orphan	:	A child whose parents are dead.
Panacea	:	A cure for all diseases.
Pathology	:	Science of diseases.
Patricide	:	The murder of one's own father.
Patrimony	:	Property inherited from one's father or ancestors.
Patriot	:	One who defends or is zealous for one's own country's freedom or rights.
Patron	:	Person who gives encouragement, moral or financial support to a person, cause, etc.
Pedestrian	:	One who walks.
Pessimist	:	One who looks at the dark side of things.
Pesticide	:	A substance used to kill destructive insects or animals.
Philanthropist	:	One who loves and works for his fellow men.
Physician	:	One who prescribes medicine.
Planetarium	:	Building with a device for representing the movements of the stars and planets by projecting spots of light on the inner surface of a large dome that represents the sky.
Polygamy	:	The practice of having more than one wife at the same time.
Polygon	:	A figure with many angles or sides.
Posthumous	:	A child born after the death of his father or a book published after the death of its author.
Radio	:	A receiving set which receives sound waves and changes them back to sounds or signals without the help of wires.
Recluse	:	A person who lives alone and avoids other people.
Regicide	:	The murder or murderer of a king.
Republic	:	A state in which the Government is carried on nominally, and usually in fact also, by the people or their elected representatives without a monarch.
Retaliate	:	Give tit for tat, repay an injury, wrong or injustice.

Sanitorium	:	A place with a good climate for invalids.
Sceptic	:	One who is given to questioning the truth of facts and the soundness of inferences.
Secular	:	Government in which no distinction is made between persons of different religions.
Simultaneous	:	Occurring at the same time.
Sinecure	:	An office without any work but with high pay.
Spendthrift	:	A person who spends his money recklessly.
Spokesman	:	One who speaks for others.
Stoic	:	A person who is indifferent to pleasure or pain.
Suicide	:	The taking of one's own life, or one who takes his own life.
Surgeon	:	One who uses a knife to cure a patient.
Synonym	:	A word having the same meaning.
Teetotaller	:	One who totally abstains from alcoholic drinks.
Theist	:	One who believes in the existence of God.
Thermometer	:	An instrument for measuring temperature.
Transparent	:	Allowing the passage of rays of light.
Unanimous	:	All of one mind.
Universal	:	Belonging to all parts of the world.
Usurer	:	One who lends money at exorbitant rates of interest.
Vade-mecum	:	A small handbook which can be carried about and used for reference.
Vegetarian	:	One who lives on vegetables.
Veteran	:	One who has grown old in service or has had long experience of service or occupation.
Voluntary	:	Of one's own free will.
Widow	:	A woman whose husband is dead.
Widower	:	A man whose wife is dead.
Wireless or Radio	:	Method of sending messages without the help of wires.
Zoology	:	Science of the life of animals.

EXERCISE

Express the following single words in groups of words:
Anniversary, antiquarian, apostate, aquatic, ascetic, bigamy, biography, carnivore, credulous, dictatorship, emissary, fastidious, forgery, gullible, honorary, inevitable, inviolable, laxative, manuscript, mesalliance, nursery, obsolete, odalisque, patrimony, patron, pesticide, posthumous, sinecure, teetotaller, transparent, widower.

5
WORDS OFTEN CONFUSED

There are some words in English which are likely to confound the learner owing to the similarity in spelling and pronunciation. Such words create a great deal of confusion in the mind of the learner. Very often it is found that he falls into the habit of using these similar words wrongly and supposes the meaning of these words to be the same. Therefore, adequate care must be taken to distinguish the one from the other. Some pairs of words that look similar in pronunciation and spelling are entirely different in meaning from each other. A list of words likely to be confused is as follows:

	Similar Words		Different usage
1.	Access	-	*To be easy to approach.* Students must have access to good books. Only high officials had access to the Emperor.
	Excess	-	*Too much.* Don't carry your grief to excess. She is generous to excess.
2.	Accept	-	*Take what is offered or given.* Rama accepted my proposal. Suresh Babu cannot accept you as his assistant.
	Except	-	*Excluding leaving out.* He gets up early everyday except Sunday. Nobody was late except you.
3.	Accidence	-	*Rules of grammar dealing with the changes in the forms of words.* The traditional grammar book provides information on accidence and syntax.
	Accident	-	*Something that happens without a cause that can be seen at once.* There have been many railway accidents this year.

4. Accomplice- *Helper or companion.* He committed the act of murder with the help of his accomplice.

   Accomplish- *Perform, finish successfully.* He is a man who will never accomplish anything.

5. Adapt - *To change or adjust.* When you go to a new country, you must adapt yourself to new manners and customs.

   Difficult books are often adapted for use in schools.

   Adopt - *To choose, take up or use as one's own.* As they had no children of their own, they adopted an orphan.

   He cannot decide on the course to adopt.

   Adept - *Skilled.* You are not adept at photography.

6. Affect - *Have an effect on.* The climate affected his health.

   Pretended. He affected not to hear me.

   Effect - *Result, outcome.* The children were suffering from the effect of the hot weather.

   To bring about, accomplish. The Minister of Health wants to effect a radical change in the prevailing Health Programme.

7. Affection - *Fond and tender feeling.* You have no affection for your brother.

   Affectation- *Show, pretence.* There was much affectation in his manners.

   Always keep clear of all affectation.

8. Allusion - *Indirect reference.* That man has a glass eye but he doesn't like people to make any allusion to it.

   There is an allusion to Helen of Troy in this passage.

   Illusion - *Something that does not really exist, deceptive appearance.* I have no illusions about his ability.

   He cherishes the illusion that everyone admires him.

9. Altar - *An elevated place of worship.* They all knelt down before the altar.

   Alter - *Change.* You have to alter your plan.

10. Air   -   Let's go out and have some fresh air.
    Heir   -   *A person with the legal right to receive a title,
                     property, etc., when the owner dies.* He is heir to
                     a large fortune.

11. Alteration   -   *Change.* Some alterations have been made in
                     the second edition of the book.
    Altercation- *Quarrel, noisy argument.* He had an
                     altercation with his friend.

12. Alternate   -   *Occurring by turns.* He alternated kindness
                     with severity.
    Alternative- *One of the two things that may be used or had in
                     place of something else, or choice between two
                     things.* There is no alternative to what you
                     propose.

13. Assay   -   *Test the purity of a metal.* Make an assay of an
                     ore.
    Essay   -   *Piece of writing, usually short and in prose on
                     any one subject.* He wrote an essay on the
                     current political problem of the country.

14. Assent   -   *Agreement.* The President gave his assent to
                     the Bill passed by the Parliament.
                     You should give your assent to this proposal.
    Ascent   -   *Upward movement.* The ascent of the
                     mountain was not difficult.

15. Amiable   -   *Lovable .* He is an amiable person.
    Amicable   -   *Friendly.* The land dispute was decided in an
                     amicable way.
                     Both the parties came to an amicable
                     settlement.

16. Antic   -   *Queer, odd.* Your dress and gestures are very
                     antic.
    Antique   -   *Belonging to the distant past, old.* He has an
                     antique wall clock.

17. Apposite   -   *Appropriate.* Your remarks are not apposite
                     to the points at issue.
    Opposite   -   *Front to front, contrary.* His house is situated
                     on the opposite side of the road.
                     There is a temple opposite to the hospital.

18.	Aspire	-	*Be filled with high ambition.* All great men aspire after knowledge.
	Expire	-	*To die.* His father expired last night.
19.	Auger	-	*Carpenter's tool for boring large holes in a wooden instrument for boring.* The carpenter is making holes in the beam with his auger.
	Augur	-	*Foretell.* Does this news augur war?
20.	Aught	-	*Anything.* Have you aught to say against me?
	Ought	-	*Should.* We ought to follow the traffic rules.
21.	Bail	-	*Money or credit given to get an arrested person released.* The accused was released on bail.
	Bale	-	*Large bundle of goods packed ready for transport.* Cloth is packed in bales.
22.	Balk	-	*Hinder, refuse to go forward, hesitate.* He balked his friend's plans. The horse balked at the high hedge. Her husband balked at the expenditure she had made.
	Bulk	-	*Quantity, volume.* Tankers are used to carry petroleum in bulk. He left the bulk of his property to his brother.
23.	Bare	-	*Uncovered, naked.* He never goes out with his head bare. He was bare to the waist. He fought with bare hands.
	Bear	-	*Large heavy animal with thick, rough fur; to endure.* The bear does not touch a dead body. I cannot bear that man.
24.	Beach	-	*Seashore.* They were walking along the beach.
	Beech	-	*A kind of tree.* His garden abounds in beech trees.
25.	Birth	-	*To be born, a beginning.* Birth is sure to be followed by death.
	Berth	-	*A sleeping place in a train.* He has reserved a first-class berth.
26.	Bough	-	*Large branch from the trunk of a tree.* The birds were found sitting on the boughs of the tree.
	Bow	-	*A device for shooting arrows; a decorative knot; to bend.* The tribals use bows and arrows to kill the animals.

She has a bow of pink ribbon on her hair.
They bowed down to the idol.
They bowed their heads in prayer.

27. Bridal   - *Of marriage.* He invited me to the bridal ceremony of his brother.

    Bridle   - *An instrument used to control a horse?* He took the bridle in his hand and rode on merrily.

28. Bury   - *To place a dead body in the ground and cover with earth.* He was buried at sea.

    Berry   - *Small seedy fruit.* Give the baby a few black berries.

29. Bus   - *Public conveyance that takes passengers along a fixed route.*
                They travel by bus every day.

    Boss   - *Master.* Who is the boss in this house? He wants to boss over all the workers. He wants to be the boss of the show.

30. Canon   - *General standard or principle by which something is judged.* You must accept the canons of morality.

    Cannon   - *Large, heavy gun.* The loud report of the cannon startled the soldiers.

31. Canvas   - *A piece of coarse cloth.* The bag is made of canvas.

    Canvass - *Solicit votes.* He is canvassing for votes.

32. Call   - *To make a brief visit.* I called upon him to keep his promise.

    Cull   - *Pick, select.* He used some extracts culled from the best authors.

33. Casual   - *Occasional.* He applied for casual leave for five days.

    Causal   - *Pertaining to a cause.* There is a causal connection between the two events.

34. Coarse   - *Rough.* He wears a dress made of coarse cloth. I do not like his coarse manners.

    Course   - *Onward movement of direction or time.* The railway is in the course of construction.
                Sow the seed and in due course you will have flowers.

35.	Cot	-	*Narrow bed.* There is a fine cot in his drawing room.
	Cut	-	*To divide into parts with a sharp-edged instrument.* He cut a slice of cake for his friend.
36.	Ceiling	-	*The inner roof.* The ceiling of the house should be whitewashed.
	Sealing	-	*Stamping as a mark of genuineness; closing tightly and securely.* Sealing of the ballot boxes was done after the polling hour was over.
37.	Celebrate	-	*To mark a happy occasion with any pleasurable activity.* He celebrated his birthday with much pomp and ceremony.
	Celibate	-	*Unmarried person.* He was a celibate.
38.	Cession	-	*Give up rights or land, etc., to somebody or to another state.* India demanded the cession of a part of the State.
	Session	-	*Meeting of a law court, law-making body, etc.* The new academic session of the colleges usually starts sometime in the first week of July.
39.	Cease	-	*Stop.* The old German Empire ceased to exist in 1918. The factory has ceased making bicycles.
	Seize	-	*Take hold of.* Seize a thief by the collar. The bank seized his property for non-payment of debt.
40.	Cell	-	*Small room.* Nehru lived for fourteen and a half months in a cell in the Dehradun gaol.
	Sell	-	*To give in exchange for money.* Will you sell me your car?
	Sale	-	*The act of selling.* The sale of his old home made him sad.
41.	Check	-	*Examine; stop or prevent.* He checked his enemy's advance. Your extravagant spending must be checked. Will you please check these figures?
	Cheque	-	*A written order to a bank to pay amount from an account.* He gave me a cheque on the State Bank.

42. Choir   - *A chorus.* The prayer song was sung by a choir.

    Coir   - *The fibre of the husk of the coconut.* Door mats are usually made of coir.

43. Cite   - *Quote.* He cited a few lines from T.S. Eliot.

    Site   - *A place chosen for any particular purpose.* They selected a site for a new college.

    Sight   - *View.* We are not yet within sight of the end of this wearisome task.
                 They have lost sight of their friends.

44. Collision - *Come together violently.* There was a collision between a bus and a taxi.

    Collusion - *Secret understanding or agreement for a wrong purpose.* There is a collusion between Nitish and Harish who appear to be opposed to each other.
                 He acted in collusion with his friend.

45. Colour   - *Reflection of light waves of various lengths.* There is not enough colour in the picture. Red, blue and yellow are colours.

    Collar   - *Part of a garment that fits round the neck.* The wind was so cold that he turned his coat collar up.
                 Seize by the collar. The policeman collared the thief.

46. Coat   - *Outer garment with sleeves.* He wears a woollen coat in the winter season.
                 Layer of paint put on a surface at one time. The woodwork has had its final coat of paint.

    Court   - *Place where law cases are heard.* The prisoner was brought to court for trial.

47. Compliment- *An expression of regard.* Tender my best compliments to your parents.

    Complement- *That which makes something complete.* Justice and mercy are complements of each other.

48. Condemn   - *To declare to be utterly wrong.* They condemned the authoritative attitude of their boss.

    Contemn   - *To hate, despise.* Little things should not be contemned.

49. Confident - *One who has faith in himself.* He is confident of his success in the Bank examination.

   Confidant - *A person who is trusted with private affairs or secrets.* Your confidant will not betray your secrets.

50. Conform - *Be in agreement with, comply with.* You should conform to the rules. One should conform to certain principles in one's life.

   Confirm - *Make opinions, rights, feelings, etc., stronger.* Please confirm your telephone message by letter.
   What you tell me confirms my suspicions.

51. Console - *Bracket to support a shelf.* The narrow table is held up by a console against the wall.

   Console - *Give comfort or sympathy to somebody who is unhappy.* He consoled himself with the thought that it might have been worse.
   They consoled him for his loss.

   Consul - *State's agent living in a foreign country.* The Government of India has appointed consuls in different countries of the world.

52. Continuous- *Going on without a break.* There was a continuous shower of rain for four hours.

   Continual - *Going on all the time without stopping or with only short breaks.*
   Aren't you tired of this continual rain?

   Continuation - *Continuing, starting again after a stop.*
   Continuation of study after the holidays was difficult at first.
   The May issue of the magazine will contain an exciting continuation of the story.

   Continuity - *The state of being continuous.* There is no continuity of subject in a dictionary.

53. Cord - Do not pull the bell cord to start the car.
   He injured his spinal cord when he fell from the roof.

   Chord - The diameter is the largest of the chords of a circle.

54. Corps   - *One of the technical branches of an army.* The
                 USA sent a fine corps of troops to the Gulf
                 region.

    Corpse   - *Dead body.* The corpse is usually taken to the
                 cremation ground to be burnt there.

55. Corporal   - *Of the body.* Corporal punishment is wrongly
                 given to young students.
                 The criminal was given corporal punishment
                 by the police.

    Corporeal - *Having a body.* Ghosts are not corporeal
                 beings.

56. Council   - *Group of persons appointed or elected to give
                 advice.* He is a member of the municipal
                 council.

    Counsel   - *Advice.* Keep your own counsel.
                 Consult. You should hold counsel with your
                 friend.

57. Deference - *Regard.* They treated him with deference.

    Difference - *Dissimilarity.* There is little difference
                 between the two.

58. Dear   - *Loved, lovable.* Your mother is dear to you.
                 What a dear little child.
                 Highly priced. Everything is getting dearer.

    Deer   - *Graceful and quickly moving animal.* The male
                 deer has horns.

59. Dependent- *Depending on.* The man was out of work and
                 dependent upon his son's earnings.
                 Promotion is dependent upon your record of
                 success.

    Dependant- *Somebody who depends upon another or others
                 for a home, food, etc.*
                 You should not abandon your dependants to
                 their fate.

60. Depository- *Storehouse.* You can find this book in the
                 depository.

    Depositary- *A person with whom anything is deposited.* The
                 woman left her ornaments with her
                 depositary (trustee).

61. Deprecate - *Feel and express disapproval of.* Hasty action is to be deprecated.

He deprecates changing the rules at present.

Depreciate - *Make or become less in value.* The purchasing power of money has depreciated since he bought his savings certificates.

Do not depreciate my efforts to help.

62. Descent - *Coming or going down.* The descent of the mountain took two hours.

He traced his descent from a noble family.

Decent - *Right and suitable; respectable.* Put on some decent clothes before you call on your friends. Poor people cannot always live in decent conditions.

He is a very decent fellow (likeable).

Dissent - *Have a different opinion from, refuse to assent to.* I strongly dissent from what the last speaker has said.

63. Discomfort- *Absence of comfort; uneasiness of mind or body.* The heat of summer is always a great discomfort.

Discomfit - *Upset the plans of; confuse.* Saddam Hussein was quite discomfited by the combined attack of the multinational troops.

64. Disease - *Sickness.* He suffered from a dangerous disease.

Decease - *Death.* The sudden decease of his father shocked him greatly.

65. Draft - *A rough sketch.* You should make a draft of the letter.

Draught - *Current of air in a room.* You will catch cold if you sit in a draught.

Drought - *Continuous dry weather causing distress, want of rain.* The drought caused the failure of crops.

Drat - *(Used only in exclamations) confound; curse; bother.* Drat that child!

66. Dying - *About to die.* The dying man spoke the truth.

Dyeing - *Colouring.* His sister is an expert in dyeing.

67. Elicit   - *To draw out; cause to come out.* The police started beating the accused to elicit the truth from him.

    Illicit   - *Unlawful; forbidden.* The man was tried in the court of law for the illicit sale of opium.

68. Eligible - *Fit to be chosen.* You are eligible for the post.

    Illegible - *Difficult to read.* His handwriting is illegible.

69. Elusive   - *Tending to elude or escape.* He used an elusive word in the sentence.

                His language is quite elusive.

    Illusive - *Deceptive.* The light he was following was illusive.

70. Emend   - *Take out errors from.* Emend the passage in the book.

    Amend   - *Improve, free from faults or errors.* You should amend your erring ways.

    Amends   - *Give compensation.* Avinash made amends to Bimal for the injury he caused him.

71. Emigrant - *One who leaves one's own country and goes to live in another.* Emigrants from India once settled in Japan.

    Immigrant - *One who comes into a country from another in order to live there.* In India the immigrants enjoy equal rights with the Indians themselves.

72. Eminent   - *Distinguished.* His friend is a man of eminent goodness.

                His brother is an eminent scholar.

    Imminent - *Likely to come or happen soon.* A storm is imminent.

                He was faced with imminent death.

                He is in imminent danger.

73. Ensure   - *Make safe or sure.* I cannot ensure his being there in time.

                We cannot ensure success. I cannot ensure you a good post.

    Insure   - *Make a contract that promises to pay, secure payment of a sum of money in case of accident, damage, loss, etc.* Insurance companies will insure ships and their cargoes against loss at sea.

Insure your house against fire.

74. Eruption - *Outbreak of a volcano.* There was a terrible eruption of the volcano.

    Irruption - *Sudden and violent entry.* The irruption of Mahmud of Ghazni was a notable event in the history of India.

75. Faint - *Weak, indistinct, not clear.* The sounds of music grew fainter in the distance.
She called for help in a faint voice.
There was a faint smell of incense in the temple.

    Feint - *Pretence.* He made a feint of reading the book. His smile was but a feint to deceive us.

76. Fair - *Bright, free from blemish, trade show.* Everyone must have a fair share.
He has a fair chance of success.
The girl has a fair complexion.
He visited the village fair.

    Fare - *Money charged for a journey; passenger in a hired vehicle; progress, get on.*
The bus fare from Bhubaneswar to Cuttack is Rs. 5.
The taxi driver had only six fares all day.
How did you fare during your journey?
It has fared well with him.

77. Felicity - *Happiness.* The virtuous can enjoy true felicity.

    Facility - *Opportunity, skill.* He has a great facility in learning languages.
He was lucky to get every facility for higher education.

78. Funeral - *Burial or burning of a dead person with the usual religious ceremonies.* They attended the funeral ceremony.

    Funereal - *Pertaining to funeral, gloomy, dark.* You can mark a funereal expression on his face.

79. Gait - *Manner of walking.* An awkward gait causes annoyance.

    Gate - *Opening in the wall of a city, hedge, fence, or other enclosure.* He opened the garden gate.
He jumped over the gate into the field.

80. **Gall** - *Humiliate.* He galled them with his ironical remarks.

    Gull - *A kind of large bird; cheat.* Gulls are long-winged sea-birds.
    They gulled him out of his money.

81. **Gamble** - *To play games of chance for money.* He lost his money gambling at cards.
    He has gambled away half his fortune.

    Gambol - *Quick, playful, jumping or skipping movement.* The girl was gambolling at the sight of her mother.

82. **Gentle** - *Mild, kind, friendly.* He is a man of gentle birth.
    They are all gentlemen.

    Genteel - *Polite and well-bred, elegant.* He has a genteel appearance.
    His friend's manners are quite genteel.

83. **Ghastly** - *Death-like; pale and ill.* He was looking ghastly.
    Her face was looking ghastly pale.

    Ghostly - *Pertaining to a ghost.* Vague shapes were looking ghostly in the darkness.

84. **Gilt** - *Thin layer of gold.* His sister does not like to wear gilt ornaments.

    Guilt - *Condition of having done wrong.* The guilt of the accused man was in doubt.

85. **Gird** - *Fasten with a belt.* Gird up your robe.

    Guard - *Protect; state of watchfulness against attack, danger or surprise.* The sentry is on guard.
    Be on your guard against pickpockets.
    Guard against disease.

86. **Godly** - *Pious.* He led a godly life.
    Godlike - *Like God.* He is a godlike man.

87. **Hoard** - *Carefully saved and guarded store of money, food or other treasured objects.* He came by a hoard of gold coins.

    Horde - *Wandering tribe.* The police arrested a horde of robbers.

88. **Hoarse** - *Rough and harsh voice.* He shouted himself hoarse.

	Horse	-	The horse is a helpful animal.
89.	Hot	-	I like my food hot.
			It's hot today.
	Hurt	-	*Cause bodily injury or pain.* He hurt his back when he fell.
			He was rather hurt by their criticism.
			His pride was severely hurt.
	Hut	-	*Small, roughly-made house.* He lives in a hut.
90.	Human	-	*Pertaining to mankind.* His cruelty suggests that he is less than human.
			To err is human, to forgive divine.
	Humane	-	*Tender, kind-hearted.* He is a man of humane character.
91.	Hunt	-	*Go after wild animals for food; search.* Wolves hunt in packs.
			They hunted high and low for the missing will (searched everywhere).
	Haunt	-	*Visit, be with, habitually or repeatedly; appear repeatedly.* The old castle is said to be haunted.
			If you do not help me, I'll haunt you after my death.
			A wrong-doer is constantly hunted by fear of discovery.
92.	Imprudent	-	*Rash, indiscreet.* Isn't it imprudent of you to marry while your salary is so low?
			He is an imprudent man who does not think of his future.
	Impudent	-	*Shamelessly rude, rudely disrespectful.* What an impudent rascal he is!
			He was impudent enough to call me a fool.
93.	Ingenuous	-	*Frank, open; innocent.* He made an ingenuous confession of his crime.
	Ingenious	-	*Clever and skilful.* He is an ingenious person. This is an ingenious toy.
94.	Jealous	-	*Envious.* He is jealous of me.
	Zealous	-	*Full of enthusiasm.* He is zealous in his bid to please his employer.
			He is zealous for liberty and freedom.

95. Judicial   - *Pertaining to a court of justice.* The people insisted upon a judicial inquiry into the matter.
The magistrate should carefully exercise his judicial power.
Impartial, critical. He is a man with a judicial mind.

    Judicious - *Showing or having good sense.* He is judicious in taking right decisions.

96. Jut   - *Stand out from; be out of line.* The soldier saw a gun jutting out from a bush.
The balcony juts out over the garden.

    Jot   - *Make a quick written note of.* The policeman jotted down their names and addresses.

97. Lightning - *Flash of light caused by discharge of electricity from one cloud to another.* The news spread like lightning.

    Lighting - *Giving light, being lighted.* The Municipal authorities have made arrangements for lighting the streets.

    Lightening- *Make less heavy.* Her heart lightened when she heard the news.
Make light or bright. A solitary candle lightened the darkness of the cellar.
To reduce the weight of. The accused prayed to the judge for the lightening of the sentence.

98. Loath   - *Unwilling.* He is loath to accompany his sister.

    Loathe   - *To dislike greatly.* She was sea-sick, and loathed the smell of greasy food.

99. Loose   - *Free, unbound, not tight.* That dog is too dangerous to be left loose.
He has put on a loose shirt.

    Lose   - *To misplace; unable to find.* He lost his money.
He lost two sons in the war.
Don't lose patience.
Don't lose your temper.

100. Luxuriant - *Strong in growth; abundant.* This tree has a luxuriant growth.

Luxurious - *Very comfortable.* He lives in luxurious surroundings.

101. Metal - *Any of a class of chemical elements.* Iron is a precious metal.

Mettle - *Spirit; quality of endurance or courage.* He is a man of mettle.
His horse is full of mettle.

102. Monetary - *Of money.* His monetary condition is not sound.

Monitory - *To give admonition.* Saddam Hussein neglected the monitory advice of his friends.

103. Moral - *Goodness or rightness of conduct.* You must write the moral of the poem.
He gave his friend moral support.

Morale - *State of discipline and spirit.* The army recovered its morale and fighting power.
The failing morale of the enemy helped to shorten the war.

104. Naughty - *Wicked.* He is a naughty boy.
Knotty - *Containing knots; difficult.* This is a knotty question indeed.

105. Pallet - *Straw-filled mattress for sleeping on.* He has spread a coverlet over the pallet.

Palate - *Roof of the mouth; sense of taste.* He feels much pain in the palate.
The chef has a good palate for wines.

Palette - *Board used by the artist for mixing colours.* The artist mixes his colours in a palette.

106. Pander - *Give help or encouragement to somebody, to his base passions and desires.* Sometimes newspapers pander to the public interest in crime.

Ponder - *Think over.* He pondered over the incident.

107. Pail - *Vessel for carrying liquid.* She has kept a pail of milk in the kitchen.

Pale - *Relating to a person's face, having little colour, bloodless.* He turned pale at the news.
You are looking pale today.

108. Pare - *Cut away the outer part, edge or skin of.* She pared her finger nails.

He pared the claws of his dog.

Reduce. You must pare down his expenses.

Pair   - *Two things of the same kind used together.* He went to the market to buy a pair of shoes.

109. Pat   - *Hit gently with the open hand or with something flat.* He patted his dog.

At the right moment. The answer came pat.

Pate   - *Head.* Look at the bald pate of that man.

Pet   - *Treated with care and affection.* The dog is a pet animal.

Amlan is the teacher's pet.

110. Paunch   - *Belly, especially if fat.* He was getting quite a paunch because of lack of exercise.

Punch   - *Tool or machine for cutting holes in leather, metal, paper, etc.* Punch holes in a sheet of metal.

111. Persecute   - *Punish, treat cruelly, especially because of religious belief.* There are some people who suffer persecution for their religious beliefs. Those who deviate from the established religious beliefs are likely to be persecuted.

Prosecute   - *Continue with; start legal proceedings against.* He prosecuted his higher studies. Trespassers will be prosecuted.

112. Person   - *Man, woman, or child.* Who is this person? I shall be present at the meeting in person.

Parson   - *Parish priest; any clergyman.* The parson of the church is a kind-hearted man.

113. Personal   - *Private; individual; pertaining to a person not a group.* Let's avoid being personal.

He has some personal work to do.

You should not interfere with him in his personal matters.

Personnel   - *Staff, persons employed in any work, especially public undertakings and armed forces.* He is a personnel officer in the Rourkela Steel Plant. The government provides all facilities to the army personnel.

114. Pert   - *Saucy; not showing proper respect.* He is a pert child.

Pot	-	*Glass or earthenware vessel to contain liquids or solids.* He ate a whole pot of jam.
115. Physic	-	*Medicine.* Please take a good dose of physic.
Physique	-	*Structure and development of the body.* Amalendu is a man of strong physique.
116. Piece	-	*Part or bit.* He wants a piece of paper from you. The teapot fell and was broken to pieces.
Peace	-	*State of freedom from war; refrain from disorders; quiet; calm.* India is at peace with the neighbouring countries. After a brief period of peace, war broke out again. There is a possibility of a breach of the peace in the village. Who does not want peace of mind?
117. Popular	-	*Well-liked by people.* We have a popular government in our country. Amitabh Bachchan is a popular film star. He is a man who is popular with his neighbours. *Low prices.* Meals at popular prices should be served to the poor.
Populous	-	*Thickly populated.* Delhi is a populous city.
118. Precede	-	*Come or go before.* The calm preceded the storm. He has stated his point of view in the preceding paragraph.
Proceed	-	*Go forward; continue.* Let's proceed to the next item on the agenda. Please proceed with your work. They proceeded from Cuttack to Sambalpur.
119. Precedent	-	*Earlier happening, decision, etc., taken as an example or rule for what comes later.* Is there a precedent for what you want me to do?
President	-	Shri K. R. Narayanan is the President of India. Who is the president of your party?
120. Prescribe	-	*Advise or order the use of.* What did the doctor prescribe for this illness?

The doctor prescribed a long rest.

You are required to complete the prescribed form.

Proscribe - *Publicly put (a person), out of the protection of the law; denounce as dangerous.* The government proscribed certain books this year.

121. Register - *Record or list.* Your name is not in the Register of voters.

His name is not in the register of the college.

Registrar - *Person whose duty is to keep records or registers.* The students met the Registrar of the University.

122. Righteous - *Just.* You should fight for a righteous cause.

Riotous - *Likely to cause a violent outburst of lawlessness; unruly; disorderly; running wild.* They were charged with riotous behaviour.

The police tried to control the riotous mob.

123. Rout - *Utter defeat and disorderly retreat.* The defeat became a rout.

Route - *Way taken or planned from one place to another.* The climbers tried to find a new route to the top of the mountain.

124. Sail - *Go for a sail.* There was not a sail in sight.

He has sailed for New York.

Sale - *The act of selling.* The sale of his old house made him sad.

Is the house for sale?

125. Scent - *Smell especially of something pleasant.* She uses too much scent on her hair.

Cent - Seventy per cent of the total population of India are Hindus.

126. Seize - *Take possession of property, etc., by law.* The bank authorities seized his house and other property for non-payment of debt.

The Inspector of Police seized the thief by the collar.

Siege - *Period of operation of armed forces to capture a fortified place.* The army began a siege of the city.

127. Sometime - *At a certain time.* I saw him sometime in May. *Formerly.* He was sometime professor of English, in Utkal University.

Sometimes - *Now and then.* I sometimes get letters from him.

128. Spacious - *Wide.* The rooms of his house are spacious. This is a spacious room.

Specious - *Seeming right or true but not really so.* He cannot be deceived by your specious arguments. Your specious argument cannot convince me.

129. Stationary - *Not intended to be moved from place to place; not moving or changing.* The earth is not a stationary body. The bus collided with a stationary van.

Stationery - *The articles sold by a stationer.* Ramesh has a stationery shop at New Delhi.

130. Temper - *State or condition of the mind.* He lost his temper.

Tamper - *Meddle or interfere with.* Someone has been tampering with the lock.

131. Team - *Group of people working together.* There was a match between the two teams.

Teem - *Be full off.* The lake-side teemed with gnats and mosquitoes. His head teems with bright ideas.

132. Tenor - *General routine or direction of one's life; general meaning or drift of a speech.* She knew enough Spanish to get the tenor of what was being said.

Tenure - *Period of, time of or condition of holding.* The farmers want security of tenure. The tenure of office of the president is five years.

133. Timber - *Wood prepared for use in buildings.* The fire destroyed thousands of acres of timber.

Timbre - *Characteristic quality of sound produced by a particular voice or instrument.* The timber of a sound produced by a violin is very pleasant.

134. Treatise - *Book, etc., that deals with one subject.* He wrote a treatise on ethics.

    Treaties - *Agreements between two or more countries.* The Gulf War was brought to a close by a treaty. The two nations were bound by treaties to help each other.

135. Urban - *Pertaining to a town.* The government now gives more attention to the development of urban areas.

    Urbane - *Polite, polished in manners; refinement.* We were much pleased with his urbane manners.

136. Vain - *Without value or meaning or result.* All his work was in vain.
    He tried in vain to do this work.

    Vein - *Blood passes through veins and arteries.* There are many veins in a human body.
    (Figuratively). There is a vein of melancholy in his character.

137. Veracious - *True; truthful.* A veracious man is loved and respected by all.

    Voracious - *Greedy.* Subhendu is a voracious eater.

138. Wander - *Go from place to place without any definite aim.* He wandered up and down the roadside aimlessly.
    They wandered miles and miles in the mist.
    He wandered over the countryside.

    Wonder - *Feeling caused by something unusual, surprising; surprise combined with admiration.* They were filled with wonder at the view of the majestic mountains.
    We looked at the conjurer in silent wonder.
    No wonder you were so late.

139. Wreath - *Garland.* The burning mountain in the summer season looked like a wreath of flowers from a distance.

    Wreathe - *Cover, encircle.* She wreathed a garland with these flowers.
    Wind around. The snake wreathed itself around the branch.

140. Yoke   - *Wooden bar put across necks of animals; oppressive force.* The farmer put a yoke on his two bullocks to hold them together as they ploughed.
The rebels freed the people from the yoke of the tyrant.

     Yolk   - *Yellow part of an egg.* Eat the yolk of an egg in a balanced diet.

EXERCISES

Make sentences of your own to indicate the difference in meaning between the following pairs of words:

Amend, emend; coat, court; compliment, complement; corporal, corporeal; council, counsel; dear, deer; decent, descent; deference, difference; eminent, imminent; illusive, elusive; fair, fare; gamble, gambol; genteel, gentle; gilt, guilt; haunt, hunt; jute, jot; loose, lose; pair, pare; ponder, pander; parson, person; prescribe, proscribe; seize, siege; stationary, stationery; tamper, temper; timber, timbre.

6
WORDS USED BOTH AS NOUNS AND AS VERBS

There are many words in English which can be used both as Nouns and Verbs. Since some words are not always the same part of speech, they can be used in other parts of speech. Before we say that a word is used as a Noun or as a Verb in a sentence, we must take into account the function and use of that word. It is the function of a word that distinguishes its use as a Verb from its use as a Noun. The following are some of the most important words which are used both as Nouns and Verbs:

Abandon : They were waving their arms with abandon. (N)
The cruel man abandoned his wife and child.(V)
They had abandoned all hope. (V)

Abstract : This is an abstract of a sermon. (N)
Usually the miners abstract metal from ore.
Did that man abstract a watch from your pocket? (V).

Abuse : We must try to put an end to abuse. He greeted his friend with a stream of abuses. He showered abuses on his friend. (N)
Don't abuse your authority. (V)

Accent : In the word 'today' the accent is on the second syllable. He speaks English with the right accent. (N)
In the word 'today' the second syllable is accented. (V)

Accord : He did this work of his own accord. The Mayor of the Corporation signed an accord with the workers. (N)

He was accorded a warm welcome. His behaviour does not accord with his principles. (V)

Account : I have an account with the State Bank of India. I want to open an account with a bank. Can I settle my account? (N).
He has been asked to account for his conduct. In English law a man is accounted innocent until he is proved guilty. His illness accounts for his absence (V).

Ache : He is suffering from a headache. (N)
My head aches. After climbing the mountain, he ached all over. He ached to be free. His heart aches for her. (V)

Act : It is an act of kindness to help a blind man across the street. In the act of picking up the ball, he slipped and fell. (N)
The girl's life was saved because the doctors acted so promptly. You have acted generously. Do not act the fool. (V).

Addict : He is a drug addict. (N)
He is addicted to smoking. (V)

Address : Let me know if you change your address. (N)
The Minister of Education will now address the meeting. Don't address him as 'Colonel'; he is only a Major. The letter was wrongly addressed. (V)

Advance : Nothing could stop the advance of enemy soldiers. With the advance of old age, he could no longer do the work well. Science has made great advances during the last fifty years. (N)
Our troops have advanced two miles. Has civilisation advanced during this century? The forces of the enemy advanced against us. May I advance my opinion on the matter? He worked so well that he was soon advanced to the position of a manager. The shopkeepers advanced their prices. The banks often advance money to farmers for the purchase of seed and fertilisers. (V)

Advantage : The advantages of a good education are great.
Living in a big town has many advantages,
such as good schools, libraries and theatres.
(N)
In what way will it advantage them ? (V)

Advocate : He joined the Bar as an advocate. He is a
member of the Faculty of Advocates. (N)
Do you advocate keeping all children at school
till the age of 16? (V)

Age : What is his age? At what age do children start
school in your country? His back was bent
with age. Shakespeare belonged to the
Elizabethan Age. (N).
He is ageing fast. (V)

Aid : He came to my aid. (N)
He aided his friend. (V)

Aim : He missed his aim. What is your aim in life?
(N)
He aimed his gun at the lion. My remarks
were not aimed at you. What are you aiming
at? (V)

Air : Let's go out and have some fresh air. My plans
are still quite in the air. The house has an air of
comfort. (N)
The mattress needs to be aired. He likes to air
his knowledge. (V)

Alarm : Give the alarm for six o'clock. He jumped up
in alarm. I hope you did not take alarm at the
news. (N)
The noise of the shot alarmed hundreds of
birds. Everybody was alarmed at the news
that war might break out. (V)

Answer : Foreign languages are often taught through
questions and answers. He made no answer.
(N)
He answered all questions. He answered
nothing. Have you answered his letter?
Answer this question. (V)

Appeal : He made an appeal for help. He was acquitted
on appeal. (N)

The prisoner appealed to the judge for mercy. At Christmas, people appeal to us to help the poor. Bright colours appeal to small children. (V)

Approach : The enemy ran away at our approach. (N)
As winter approached the weather became colder. Few writers can even approach Shakespeare in greatness. (V)

Array : There is a fine array of tools. (N)
The Duke and his men arrayed themselves against the King (V).

Arrest : The police made several arrests. The officer was put under arrest. (N)
Poor food arrests the natural growth of children. The bright colours of the flowers arrested the child's attention. The police arrested the thief and put him in prison. (V)

Attack : He made an attack upon his enemy. Attack is said to be the best form of defence (N).
The members in the opposition party attacked the Prime Minister's proposal. Rust attacks metals. (V)

Award : His horse was given the highest award at the show. (N)
He was awarded the first prize.
The judge awarded him five thousand rupees as damages. (V)

Awe : He had a feeling of awe as he was taken before the judge. The lazy boy stood in awe of his stern teacher. (N)
I was awed by his solemn words. He awed them into obedience. (V)

Back : If you lie on your back, you can look up at the sky. He slipped and fell on his back. (N)
The horse backed suddenly. He promised to help and then backed out. Their house backs on to our garden. He backed the car into the garage. (V)

Better : Her sense of humour got the better of her. We should respect our betters. (N)

The government hopes to better the conditions of the peasants. Your work last year was good, I hope you will better it this year. (V)

Bias : He has a bias towards the plan. He is without bias. (N)
The government used newspapers and the radio to bias the opinions of the people. (V)

Bid : Are there no bids for this very fine painting? Will no one make a higher bid? Bids were invited for the construction of a swimming pool. (N)
Will anyone bid Rs. 5000 for this painting? I hoped to get the house but a rich man was bidding against me. The politicians are bidding for popular support. (V)

Bite : His face was covered with insect bites. There is a bite in the air this morning. (N)
The dog bit him in the leg. Does your dog bite? He bit off a large piece of the apple. (V)

Blame : Where does the blame lie for our failure? You must not put the blame for the accident upon me. I always have to bear the blame. If you do not do the work well, you will incur blame. (N)
He blamed the teacher for his failure. He blamed his failure on his teacher. I have nothing to blame myself for. (V)

Blare : Do you like to listen to the blare of a brass band? (N)
The trumpets blared forth. He blared out a warning. (V)

Blast : A blast of hot air came from the furnace. When the window was opened, an icy blast came into the room. Thousands of windows were broken by blasts during the air raids in Iraq. (N)
The tree had been blasted by lightning. His hopes were blasted. (V)

Blaze : We could see the blaze of a cheerful fire through the window. I put some wood on the fire and it soon burst into a blaze. The main street of the town is a blaze of light in the evening. (N)

When the fireman arrived, the whole building was blazing. The governor's uniform blazed with gold lace. The sun blazed down on us. (V)

Blend : This coffee is a blend of Java and Brazil. They sell excellent blends of tea. (N)

A grocer must know how to blend tea. Our coffees are carefully blended. Oil and water do not blend. These two colours blend well. (V)

Blind : Please pull down the blinds. (N)

The soldier had been blinded in the war. His admiration for her beauty blinded him to her faults. (V)

Blister : If your shoes are too tight, you may get blisters on your feet. (N)

He is not used to manual work and his hands blister easily. The hot sun has blistered the paint on the door. (V)

Block : A butcher cuts up his meat on a large block of wood. The blocks of stone in the pyramids are five or six feet high. The statue is to be cut out of a block of marble. (N)

All roads were blocked by the heavy snowfall. They blocked the entrance to the cave with big rocks. (V)

Blossom : The apple trees are in blossom. (N)

The cherry trees will blossom next month. He blossomed out as a first-rate athlete. (V)

Blow : He struck his enemy a heavy blow on the head. (N)

The wind blew his hat off. The wind blew the papers out of my hand. (V)

Blush : She turned away to hide her blushes. (N)

She blushed for (with) shame. (V)

Boast : It was the enemy's boast that they could never be defeated. It was his boast that he had never failed in the examination. (N)

He boasts of being the best tennis player in the town. He often boasts to his neighbours about the successes of his children. (V)

Book   : He has written many books.

There is a book on the table. (N)

Seats for the theatre can be booked from 10 a.m. to 6 a.m. Have you booked your passage to Delhi? (V)

Border   : They camped on the border of a lake. There is a border of flowers round the lawn. (N)

Our garden is bordered by a stream. My land borders (upon) yours. The park borders on the shores of the lake. (V)

Boss   : Who is the boss in this house? (N)

He wants to boss over all his colleagues. (V)

Bother   : His lazy son is quite a bother to him. This drawer won't shut, is not it a bother? They had quite a lot of bother (in) getting here because of the fog. (N)

Do not bother me with foolish questions. That man is always bothering me to lend him money. Do not bother your head about it. (V)

Bound   : It is beyond the bounds of human knowledge. There are no bounds to his ambition. Please keep within the bounds of reason. (N)

You should bound your desires. The ball struck the wall and bounded back to me. His heart bounded with joy. (V)

Box   : Pack the books in a wooden box. (N)

The teacher got annoyed with the boy and boxed his ears. (V)

Break   : He has been writing since 2 o'clock without a break. (N)

When she dropped the teapot it broke. The boy fell from the tree and broke his leg. Glass breaks easily. (V)

Brush   : He gave his clothes a good brush. (N)

He brushed away a fly from his nose. (V)

Build   : They are of the same build. He is a man of powerful build. (N)

He built a house at Cuttack. Birds build nests. (V)

Bustle : Why is there so much bustle? (N)
Everyone was bustling about. She bustled the children off to school. (V)

Call : They came at his call. He will give a call. Please remain within call. (N)
He called to her father for help. This train calls at every station. A man has called to read the electric light meter. His name is Srikant but we call him Litu. You may call him what you like. (V)

Camp : The soldiers live in camps at the time of war. (N)
They camped out in the woods. (V)

Care : You should give more care to your work. This is made of glass, so take care not to break it. Take care (that) you do not get run over when you cross the street. Do your work with more care. (N)
He failed in the examination but I do not think he cares very much. He does not care what they say. I do not care who you are. He does not care a pin. (V)

Cast : His leg was in a plaster cast. (N)
The fisherman cast his net into the water. Snakes cast their skins. (V)

Catch : That was a difficult catch. He is a good catch for some young ladies. (N)
He threw the ball to them to catch. The dog caught the bit of meat in its mouth. How many fish did you catch? He waited to catch the boys stealing apples from his garden. (V)

Cause : The cause of the fire was carelessness. We cannot get rid of war until we get rid of the causes of war. There is no cause for anxiety. (N)
What causes the tides? You have caused trouble to all of us. This has caused us much anxiety. He caused the prisoners to be put to death. (V)

Chain : Man is born free but is everywhere in chains. (N)

The prisoners were chained to the wall. Chain up your dog. (V)

Chair : Won't you take a chair? There are so many chairs in that room. (N)
The newly elected M.P. was chaired by his supporters. (V)

Chance : Let's leave it to chance. Let chance decide. He has no chance of winning. He has had no chances to get away. (N)
I chanced to be there. It chanced that I was not at home when he called. (V)

Change : We shall have to make a change in the programme. You need a change of air. We have a new house, it is a great change for the better. There have been many changes in the village since I lived there as a boy. Let us hope there will be a change in the weather. (N)
He changed his clothes before going out. It won't take me five minutes to change. I have changed my address. Can you change this five-rupee note? Caterpillars change into butterflies or moths. The wind has changed from north to south. That has changed my ideas. (V)

Channel : The channel is marked by buoys. Keep to the channel; the river is shallow at the sides. He has secret channels of information. (N)
The river had channelled its way through the soft rock. (V)

Charge : They brought a charge of murder against him. He was arrested on a charge of theft. Meera was in charge of the baby. This ward of the hospital is in (under) the charge of Dr. Kamalesh. (N)
He was charged with murder. He charged me with neglecting my duty. Our soldiers charged the enemy. The wounded lion suddenly charged at them. (V)

Charm : Her charm of manner made her very popular. He fell a victim to her charms. (N)

		Does goodness charm more than beauty? We were charmed with the scenery. She charmed away his sorrow. (V)
Chase	:	After a long chase, the police caught the thief. (N)
		Dogs like to chase rabbits. Chase that dog out of the garden. (V)
Chat	:	He had a long chat with them. (N)
		They were chatting away in a corner. (V)
Cheat	:	He is a cheat. (N)
		He cheated all his clients shamelessly. (V)
Check	:	Wind acts as a check upon speed. They are keeping the enemy in check. (N)
		I advise you to keep a check on your temper. I will ask the waiter for my check (bill). Which pattern do you want for your new dress, a stripe or a check. (V)
Cheek	:	He had the cheek to ask me to do his work for him. No more of your cheek! (impudence) (N)
		Stop cheeking your mother! (be impudent to) (V)
Cheer	:	The players usually feel encouraged by words of cheer. (N)
		Your visit has cheered the sick man. Everyone was cheered by the good news. He was cheered by the good news. He cheered up at once when I promised to help him. The boys cheered their football team. (V)
Chill	:	There is quite a chill in the air this morning. Take the chill of the water. The bad news cast a chill over the gathering. (N)
		He was chilled to the bone. Do not chill their enthusiasm. (V)
Chime	:	There was a chime of bells. Listen to the chimes. (N)
		The bells chimed out a tune. The bells are chiming. The church clock chimed the midnight hour. (V)
Choke	:	The choke in a petrol engine usually controls the intake of air. (N)

The smoke almost choked me. Her voice was choked with sobs. Anger choked his words. (V)

Circle : He has a large circle of friends. They are newcomers to our circle. The boys are standing in a circle. (N)
The aircraft circled over the landing field. The news circled round. (V)

Claim : His claim to own the house is invalid. He set up a claim to the throne. (N)
Every citizen in a democratic country may claim the protection of the law. He claimed to be the owner of the land. He claimed to have done the work without help. (V)

Clang : The clang of the firebell alarmed the village. (N) .
The tram-driver clanged his bell. (V)

Clatter : The boys stopped their clatter when the teacher came into the classroom. (N)
Pots and pans were clattering in the kitchen. Do not clatter your knives and forks. (V)

Close : Day had reached its close. The ceremony has come to a close. (N)
He could not close his door against them.
If you close your eyes, you cannot see. Many flowers open in the morning and close at night. (V)

Cloud : The top of the mountains was covered with clouds. Large black clouds announced a coming storm. (N)
The sky clouded over. Her eyes were clouded with tears. All these troubles have clouded his mind. (V)

Collapse : His father suffered a nervous collapse. (N)
The roof collapsed under the weight of snow. If you cut the ropes of a tent, it will collapse. (V)

Collar : The wind was so cold that he turned his coat collar up. (N)
The policeman collared the thief (seized by the collar). (V)

Colour	:	Red, blue, and yellow are colours. His story has some colour of truth. They attacked their opponents under the colour of patriotism. (N) News is often coloured. Traveller's tales are often highly coloured. (V)
Comfort	:	He became fond of comfort as he grew old. His friend is living in great comfort. Your letters have been a great comfort for me. The hotel has every modern comfort. (N) The child ran to its mother to be comforted. The insurance money comforted her after the tragic death of her husband. (V)
Command	:	His commands were quickly obeyed. He issued a command for the prisoners to be set free. He has fifty men under his command. (N) The officer commanded his men to fire. The pirate chief commanded that the prisoners should be shot. God commands and man obeys. (V)
Comment	:	Have you any comments to make upon my book? (N) They commented upon his strange behaviour. (V)
Compound	:	Common salt is a compound of sodium and chloride. (N) He compounded with his creditors for a remission of what he owed. (V)
Concern	:	Mind your own concerns. It's no concern of mine. (N) Do not trouble about things that do not concern you. He is said to be concerned in the crime. Does this concern you? (V)
Condition	:	Ability is one of the conditions of success in life. Her parents allowed her to go, but made it a condition that she should get home before midnight. The condition of his health prevents him from working. (N) My expenditure is conditioned by my income. (V)
Conflict	:	There was a wordy conflict between them. There is a long-drawn-out conflict between the employers and workers. (N)

Their account of the causes of the war conflicts with ours. (V)

Conjecture : I was right in my conjectures. We had no facts, so were reduced to conjecture. (N)
It was just as I conjectured. (V)

Consent : He was chosen leader by general consent. Silence gives consent. (N)
He consented to the proposal. (V)

Contact : A rope hanging from the balloon came into contact with an electric power line. We can learn much by being brought into contact with other minds. (N)
He contacted his friend over the telephone. Where can they contact that man? (V)

Contrast : Contrast may make something appear more beautiful than it is when seen alone. The contrast between the two brothers is remarkable. Suresh's marks by contrast with Ramesh's marks were excellent. (N)
His actions contrasted badly with his promises. Contrast these imported goods with the domestic product. (V)

Cover : Some chairs are fitted with loose covers. (N)
Snow covered the ground. The floods covered large areas on both banks of the river. (V)

Cramp : The swimmer was seized with cramp and had to be helped out of the water. (N)
All these difficulties cramped his progress. (V)

Crop : The land is in crop. The land is out of crop. The farmer will have good crops this year. The Prime Minister's statement produced a crop of questions. (N)
The sheep had cropped the grass short. The beans cropped well this year. All sorts of difficulties cropped up (arose unexpectedly). (V)

Crowd : There were large crowds of people in the streets on New Year's Eve. He pushed his way through the crowd. (N)

The pupils crowded round the teacher to ask questions. People quickly crowd round when there is a street accident. Let's not crowd the room with furniture. Memories crowded in my mind. (V)

Crush : There was a frightful crush at the gate into the stadium. (N)
Several people were crushed to death as they tried to escape from the burning theatre. Do not crush this box; it has flowers in it. (V)

Cut : I do not like the cut of this coat. There is a deep cut in his leg. That remark was a cut at him (directed). (N)
We cut paper and cloth with scissors. He cut his face while shaving. The pages of some books need to be cut. Please cut a slice of cake for her. (V)

Dart : The child made a sudden dart across the road. (N)
The deer darted away when it saw them. The snake darted out its tongue. She darted an angry look at him. (V)

Date : What is the date today? Has the date for the meeting been fixed? His date of birth is March 27th, 1940. (N)
Do not forget to date your letters. The letter is dated April 20th, New Delhi. (V)

Dawn : He works from dawn till dark. It's almost dawn. The war ended and we looked forward to the dawn of happier days. (N)
The day was just dawning. The truth began to dawn upon him. (V)

Deal : He has had to spend a good deal of money on medicines. I have spent a good deal of trouble over the work. (N)
The money must be dealt out fairly. Who dealt the cards? Do you deal with that thief? You must deal carefully with this problem. (V)

Decrease : There has been a decrease in our imports this year. (N)

		Your hunger decreases as you eat. The population of the village has decreased to 1000. (V)
Delight	:	She looked a dream of delight. To his great delight, he passed the examination with first class honours. He often thinks of the delights of life in the country. (N)
		Her singing delighted everyone. I was delighted to hear of his success. He delights to prove his brother wrong. He delights in teasing his young sister. (V)
Demand	:	It is impossible to satisfy all your demands. There is a great demand for typists but a poor demand for clerks. There is little demand for these goods. (N)
		Naresh demanded an apology from Nirmal. The policeman demanded his name and address. This sort of work demands great patience. (V)
Despair	:	He gave up the attempt in despair. He was filled with despair when he read the examination questions. This boy is the despair of all his teachers. (N)
		His life was despaired of. (V)
Detail	:	Please give me all the details. Do not omit a single detail. Every detail of her dress was perfect. (N)
		The boys listened breathlessly as the sailor detailed the story of the shipwreck. Three soldiers were detailed to guard the bridge (appointed). (V)
Discredit	:	If you continue to behave in this way, you will bring discredit upon yourself. His private information throws serious discredit on the newspaper accounts of the event. (N)
		His theories were discredited by the scientists. The judge advised the jury to discredit the evidence of one of the witnesses. Such foolish behaviour will discredit him with the public. (V)

Disgust : He turned away in disgust. To her great disgust, she was given a minor part in the play. His disgust at the government's policy caused him to resign. (N)
His behaviour disgusted everybody. We were disgusted at what we saw. (V)

Doubt : I have no doubt that you will succeed. There is not much doubt about his guilt. (N)
You cannot doubt your own existence. I doubt the truth of this report. Do you doubt my word? (V)

End : What is at the end of that street? That's the end. His hair stood on end. (N)
The road ends here. Let us end our quarrel. (V)

Escape : Escape from Tihar Jail is difficult. I congratulate you on your escape from the accident. (N)
Two of the prisoners have escaped from prison. His name escapes me for the moment (I cannot recall). (V)

Esteem : He lowered himself in our esteem by his foolish behaviour. We all have the greatest esteem for you. They held him in high esteem. (N)
He esteemed your father greatly. I esteem it a privilege to address this audience. (V)

Estimate : I hope the builders don't exceed their estimate. I do not know enough about him to form an estimate of his abilities. (N)
The firm estimated the cost of the new house at 3 lakhs. Ask a contractor to estimate for the repair of the building. (V)

Exchange : There have been numerous exchanges of views between the two governments. Exchange of prisoners during a war is unusual. (N)
The two drunken men exchanged hats. The two girls exchanged places. (V)

Exercise : The doctor advised him to take more exercise. The exercise of patience is essential in diplomatic negotiations. (N)

He exercises himself while fencing. You do not exercise enough. He exercised his power over his subordinates. (V)

Exhibit : There is a fine exhibit of Chinese porcelain in the museum. (N)
They exhibited great powers of endurance during the climb. (V)

Experience : His experience in life taught him nothing. He has not enough experience for this post. (N)
He experienced a good deal of trouble in life. He experienced financial hardships all through his life. (V)

Eye : He is blind in one eye. He lost an eye in the war. He opened his eyes. (N)
He eyed me with suspicion. They were eyeing us jealously. (V)

Face : He fell on his face. The stone struck him on the face. Her face is her fortune. (N)
Turn round and face me. The window faces the street. (V)

Fall : There was a heavy fall of rain yesterday. There was a fall in the prices of essential commodities. The fall of an apple caused Newton to discover the laws of gravity. (N)
He fell into the water. The book fell from the table to the floor. (V)

Fatigue : Several men dropped with fatigue during the long march. (N)
He was feeling fatigued. (V)

Favour : He obtained his position by favour more than by merit and ability. (N)
A teacher should not favour any of his pupils. Miss Sheila will now favour us with a song. (V)

Feel : You can tell it's silk by the feel. Let me have a feel. (N)
The doctor felt his pulse. Just feel the weight of this box. He felt in his pocket for some money. (V)

Fight : It is interesting to see the fights between dogs. The news that their leader had surrendered took all the fight out of them. (N)

	When dogs fight, they use their teeth. Great Britain fought against Germany in two wars. (V)
File	: They have placed the correspondence in their files. (N)
	Please file these letters. (V)
Find	: I made a great find in a second-hand bookshop the other day. (N)
	Did you ever find that pen you lost? They dug 20 feet and then found water. I can find nothing new on this subject. (V)
Fit	: She almost had a fit when she saw the bill. He committed murder in a fit of anger. (N)
	This coat does not fit me. The key does not fit the lock. (V)
Flame	: The house was in flames. (N)
	Make the fire flame up. His face flamed with anger. (V)
Flare	: The wrecked ship was using flares to attract the attention of the coastguards. (N)
	The candle began to flare. She flares up at the least provocation. (V)
Flow	: The tide is on the flow. (N)
	The tears flowed from her eyes. (V)
Foil	: A plain old woman serves as a foil to a beautiful young woman. (N)
	He foiled their plans. (V)
Foot	: A dog has four feet. He rose to his feet. (N)
	They missed the last bus, and had to foot it. The various items foot upto Rs. 1000 (add upto).
Frame	: Sobs shook her frame. (N)
	The child is framing well. The police framed a chargesheet against him. (V)
Function	: He attended all functions held in the college during the academic session. (N)
	The telephone was not functioning. Some English adverbs function as adjectives. (V)
Fuss	: Do not make so much fuss about trifles. You are making a great fuss of me. (N)

She fussed about, unable to hide her impatience. Do not fuss over the children so much. (V)

Gain	: He is interested only in gain. (N) What gained him so much reputation? This watch neither gains nor loses time. (V)
Glance	: He took a glance at the newspaper headlines. He saw so many flowers at a glance. (N) She glanced shyly at him from behind her fan. He glanced at the columns. (V)
Grace	: She danced with grace. He did the favour with a good grace. (N) The occasion was graced by the presence of the Vice-Chancellor. Her character is graced with every virtue. (V)
Grasp	: He has a thorough grasp of that problem. This problem is within my grasp. (N) A man who grasps at too much may lose everything. He could grasp the subject matter very easily. (V)
Grip	: He possesses the ability to have a good grip on an audience. (N) The frightened child gripped her mother's hand. (V)
Grudge	: He has a grudge against you. He owes that man a grudge. I bear him no grudge. (N) I do not grudge him his success. His cruel master grudged him even the food he ate. (V)
Guard	: The sentry is on guard. Be on your guard against pickpockets. (N) You must guard against disease. (V)
Guide	: Instinct is not always a good guide. He is a guide in the National Museum . (N) You must guide him properly. He was guided by his teacher. (V)
Halt	: The officer called a halt. The train came to a halt. (N) The officer halted his troops for a rest. (V)
Hand	: He lives close at hand. The examinations are at hand. I did not expect such unkind treatment at your hands. (N)

		Please hand me that book. He has handed in his resignation. (V)
Hang	:	I do not care a hang. I do not quite get the hang of your argument. (N)
		Hang your coat on that hook. A dog's tongue hangs out when it runs fast. (V)
Head	:	They cut his head off. Hit him on the head. (N)
		Manish's name headed the list of successful candidates. (V)
Help	:	Can't I be of any help? Thank you for your kind help. (N)
		I helped him find his things. Don't tell him more than you can help. (V)
Hit	:	The new play is quite a hit. That was a hit directed at him. (N)
		Hit a man on the head. They hit it off well. He hit upon a new plan. (V)
Hold	:	He has a great hold over his younger brother. (N)
		He held the knife between his teeth while swimming. Hold your head up. (V)
Honour	:	One should show honour to one's parents. May I have the honour of your company at dinner? (N)
		Will you honour him with a visit? They honoured him highly. (V)
House	:	New houses are going up everywhere. He had bought a new house. (N)
		He can house you and your friends if the hotels are full. (V)
Hurt	:	I intended no hurt to his feelings. (N)
		He was more frightened than hurt. He was rather hurt by their criticisms. (V)
Iron	:	Iron is a useful metal. (N)
		The washerman ironed my shirts. (V)
Itch	:	Do you have an itch? He has had an itch for money. (N)
		Scratch where it itches. Scratch yourself if you itch. (V)
Jam	:	Traffic jams are frequently to be found at Bhubaneswer. He got into a jam. (N)

		The logs jammed in the river. The brakes jammed and the car skidded badly. (V)
Jar	:	He has a jar of strawberry jam. The fall from his horse gave him a nasty jar. It was an unpleasant jar to my nerves. (N)
		The way in which he laughs jars on me. He was badly jarred by the blow. (V)
Job	:	He has made a good job of it. He has a job as a bus-conductor. He's out of a job. (N)
		He jobbed his brother into a well-paid post. (V)
Judge	:	He says the diamonds are not genuine; but then, he is no judge. (N)
		God will judge all men. (V)
Kick	:	The bruise was caused by a kick. (N)
		The horse kicks. The baby was kicking and screaming. (V)
Knock	:	He got a nasty knock on the head when he fell. I heard a knock at the door. (N)
		He knocked the bottom out of the box. He knocked his head on (against) the wall. Someone is knocking at the door. (V)
Last	:	His misery will not last long. (N)
		We shall fight to the last. (V)
Laugh	:	We have had a good many laughs over his foolishness. (N)
		The jokes made everyone laugh. It is unkind to laugh at a person who is in trouble. (V)
Lead	:	Keep your dog on the lead in these busy streets. Who takes the lead of the strike? (N)
		Their guide led them through a series of caves. (V)
Let	:	I want to put up my house to let. (N)
		Her father will not let her go to the dance. (V)
Light	:	We need more light. The light began to fail. (N)
		The streets were brightly lit up. Our houses are lighted by electricity. (V)
Long	:	The work won't take long. Shall you be away for long? (N)

She longed for him. The children are longing for holidays. (V)

Lump : Get out of my way, you big fat lump of a man! He broke a piece of coal into small lumps. (N) The boys agreed to lump the expenses of their camping holiday. Can we lump all these items together under the heading 'incidental charges'? (V)

Lunch : They were at lunch when I called. (N) He lunched at the Hotel Kalinga. (V)

Man : Manners show the man. (N) All the ships were adequately manned. (V)

Make : Fans of the best quality and make are sold here. (N) Make hay while the sun shines. (V)

Mark : Who made these dirty marks on my new book? Please accept this gift as a mark of my esteem. He does not feel quite upto the mark. (N) The teacher marked the pupil absent. A zebra is marked with stripes. Mark my words. What are the qualities that mark a good leader? (V)

Master : He has made himself a master of the language. He is the master of a large fortune. (N) You should master your temper. He has mastered the French language well. (V)

Match : You are no match for him. He is a good match. The football match will be held tomorrow. (N) No one can match him in archery. The carpets should match the curtains. (V)

Measure : An inch is a measure of length. A yardstick is a measure. Words cannot always give the measure of one's feelings. (N) The tailor measured him for a suit. Can you measure this table accurately? (V)

Meet : The Annual Athletic meet of the college will be held sometime in the month of February this year. (N) He met them quite by chance. Goodbye till we meet again. (V)

Mind	:	He does not know his own mind. He has made up his mind to be a doctor. No two minds think alike. (N)
		Who is minding the baby? Mind the dog. Mind your own business. If you do not mind, you will be hurt. (V)
Mirror	:	Pepys' Diary is a mirror of the times he lived in. Shakespeare's plays hold a mirror up to nature. (N)
		The still water of the lake mirrored the hillside. (V)
Miss	:	Miss Mohapatra teaches mathematics well. She is a saucy miss. That was a lucky miss (fortunate escape). A miss is as good as a mile (a narrow escape is the same in effect as an escape by a wide margin). (N)
		He missed his footing. He missed the 9.30 train and therefore, missed the accident. He missed the point of my joke. (V)
Milk	:	The milk has turned sour. (N)
		She milks the cow in the morning. (V)
Motion	:	The train was in motion. (N)
		The hermit motioned them towards him. (V)
Mouth	:	Why do you make mouths at him? He opened his mouth. (N)
		The old woman mouths her words. An actor who mouths his words is a poor actor. (V)
Move	:	Do you know all the moves in chess? There was a move towards settling the strike. Unless we make a move soon, we shall be in a hopelessly weak position. (N)
		Move your chair nearer to the wall. It was calm and not a leaf moved. We were all moved by her entreaties. The story of their sufferings moved us deeply. (V)
Name	:	What is your name? He writes under the name of Benhur. I know the man by name. (N)
		They named the child Bimalendu. The child was named after his father. Can you name all the plants and trees in this garden? (V)

Need : There is no need to start yet. There is no need for anxiety. (N)
The garden needs rain. He needs your help. It needs to be done carefully. (V)

Nod : He gave me a nod as he passed. (N)
He nodded to me as he passed. He nodded to show that he understood. He nodded approval. He nodded me a welcome. (V)

Note : He spoke for an hour without a note. There is a new edition of *Hamlet*, with copious notes. (N)
Note how to do it. She noted that his hands were dirty. The policeman noted down every word he said. (V)

Number : Number of people came from all parts of the country to see the exhibition.
A number of books are missing from the library. (N)
Let's number them from 1 to 10. We numbered 20 in all. His days are numbered (he has not long to live). (V)

Nurse : There are 20 nurses in this hospital. (N)
She nursed the child with all her affection. He nursed feelings of revenge. (V)

Object : Tell me the names of the objects in this room. He has no object in life. (N)
I object to all this noise. He stood up and objected in strong language. (V)

Occasion : This is not an occasion for laughter. He has had few occasions to speak French. (N)
The boy's behaviour occasioned his parents' anxiety. (V)

Order : He wrote their names in alphabetical order. He kept the books in order. The lift is out of order so we shall have to walk up. It is the business of the police to keep order. Some teachers find it difficult to keep order in their classes. (N)
The doctor ordered him to bed. The chairman ordered silence. The judge ordered that the prisoner should be remanded. (V)

Pain	:	He cried with pain. He felt some pain in his stomach. He worked hard and got very little for all his pains. (N)
		My foot is still paining me. I am sure your laziness pains your parents. (V)
Paint	:	He gave the doors two coats of paint. (N)
		He painted his doors and windows. (V)
Paper	:	Would you kindly give him a sheet of paper? The biology paper was difficult. The child has a paper bag. (N)
		They papered his dining-room. They charged high prices to paper the walls. (V)
Part	:	Only a part of his story is true. Parts of the book are interesting. The greater part of what you heard is only rumour. (N)
		The policeman parted the crowd. Let us part friends. On that question I am afraid I must part company with you. (V)
Pay	:	He drew his pay for the month of July. (N)
		You must pay me what you owe. I paid you the money last week. (V)
Permit	:	You won't get into the atomic research station without a permit. (N)
		Circumstances do not permit me to help you. (V)
Pinch	:	He gave her a spiteful pinch. (N)
		He pinched the boy's cheek. These shoes pinch me. (V)
Pitch	:	Excitement was raised to the highest pitch. (N)
		Let's pitch the drunkard out. The men were pitching hay. (V)
Place	:	I cannot be in two places at once. Puri is the place of Lord Jagannath. (N)
		Place them in the right order. He is a difficult man to place. I know that man's face, but I cannot place him. (V)
Plan	:	They have made plans for the holidays. (N)
		We are planning to visit new places this summer. (V)
Point	:	He was on the point of leaving. What is your point of view? (N)

	The needle of a compass points to the north. He pointed to the door. All the evidence points to his guilt. (V)
Possture	: The artist asked his model to take a reclining posture. Good posture helps you to keep well. (N) The vain girl was posturing before a tall mirror. (V)
Praise	: His heroism is worthy of great praise. He is full of praise for that man. (N) He praised that man for his courage. Their guests praised the meal as the best they had had for years. (V)
Present	: He gave his friend a beautiful present on his birthday. I will make you a present of it. (N) The criminal was presented at court. He presented a bold front to the world. The case presents some interesting features. (V)
Prick	: He feels the prick of conscience. He can still feel the prick. (N) The thorns on these roses pricked my fingers. His conscience pricked him. (V)
Pride	: His pride prevents him from doing anything dishonorable. His pride would not allow him to accept any reward. (N) He prides himself upon his skill as a great musician. (V)
Produce	: What is your agricultural produce this year? (N) The conjurer produced a rabbit from his hat. (V)
Pull	: It was a long pull to the top of the mountain. He has a strong pull with the Managing Director. (N) The horse was pulling the cart. Pull your chair to the table. (V)
Quake	: Earthquakes occasionally take place. (N) The ground quaked under his feet. He was quaking with fear. (V)
Quarrel	: He had a quarrel with his friend. (N) The thieves quarrelled with one another about how to divide the loot. (V)

Race	:	He went to the track to see the horse race. (N)
		They raced him to the station in their car. (V)
Reach	:	The grapes are beyond his reach. (N)
		They reached the aerodrome in time. (V)
Rent	:	He lives in a house free of rent. (N)
		We do not own our house, we rent it. (V)
Request	:	We came at your request. (N)
		I requested him to use his influence on my behalf. (V)
Rescue	:	You should come to the rescue of a drowning man. (N)
		He rescued the child from drowning. (V)
Rest	:	Sunday is a day of rest for many people. (N)
		We rested an hour after lunch. (V)
Reviews	:	He wrote reviews for the monthly magazines. (N)
		His new novel has been favourably reviewed. (V)
Ride	:	He went for a ride before breakfast. (N)
		He was riding fast. (V)
Rise	:	The river has its rise among the hills. (N)
		The sun rises in the east. (V)
Roll	:	He walks with a nautical roll. The young foal was enjoying a roll on the grass. (N)
		The coin fell and rolled down under the table. His debts are rolling up. (V)
Rout	:	The defeat became a rout. (N)
		They were routed out of their cabins before breakfast for a passport examination. (V)
Roof	:	The mason is working on the roof. (N)
		Roof the house with corrugated iron. (V)
Run	:	He scored sixty runs in the first innings. (N)
		The coach runs between two stations. (V)
Rush	:	I do not like the rush of city life. (N)
		The children rushed out of the school gates. (V)
Sacrifice	:	He gave his life as a sacrifice for his country. (N)
		He sacrificed his life to save the drowning child. (V)
Say	:	Let him have his say. (N)
		Everyone said how well he was looking. (V)

Second	:	The man disappeared in a second. (N)
		None seconded the resolution. (V)
Season	:	Oysters are out of season now. There are six seasons in a year. (N)
		Has this wood been well seasoned? The soldiers were not yet seasoned to the rigorous climate. (V)
Separate	:	Keep these separate from those. (N)
		Separate the good ones from the bad. (V)
Shade	:	You are so clever and brilliant that my poor efforts are thrown into the shade. (N)
		He shaded his eyes with his hand. (V)
Shape	:	My garden is in the shape of a square. (N)
		Our plans are shaping well. The boy is shaping satisfactorily. (V)
Share	:	Please let me take a share in the expenses. (N)
		He will share his last pie with me. I will share the cost with you. (V)
Shadow	:	Coming events cast their shadows before. (N)
		Two police officers shadowed the suspect. (V)
Silence	:	Speech is silver, but silence is golden. (N)
		The mother silenced her children. (V)
Skin	:	He is a wolf in a sheep's skin. (N)
		He began to skin the mangoes. (V)
Smell	:	The rose has a sweet smell. (N)
		The curry smells sour. (V)
Sort	:	He tells all sorts of cock and bull stories. (N)
		The postman was sorting out letters. (V)
Spy	:	The spy kept an eye on him. (N)
		Her mother spied footprints on the snow. (V)
Stain	:	He is a man without a stain on his character. (N)
		He stained the wood brown. The scientist stained his specimen before examining it under the microscope. (V)
Stand	:	He took his stand near the window. I take my stand upon sound precedents. (N)
		A chair will not stand on two legs. We had to stand all the way back in the bus. Do not stand there arguing about it. (V)
Start	:	He sat up with a start. The news gave me a start (surprised). He got a good start. (N)

He started at the sound of your voice. He started for America last week. (V)

Stay   : The judge granted a stay of execution. (N)
Stay where you are. I stayed to see what would happen. (V)

Strain   : Engineers calculate the strains and stresses of a bridge. Most people in the cities suffer from the strain of modern life. (N)
The wrestlers strained and struggled. (V)

Stray   : The streets were empty except for a few stray taxis. (N)
Do not stray from the point. (V)

Supply   : Have you a good supply of reading matter for the train journey? (N)
Should the government supply the need for more houses? (V)

Suspect   : Are political suspects kept under police observation in your country? (N)
I suspect him to be liar. (V)

Sweat   : They say that a good sweat will cure a cold. This job is a frightful sweat. (N)
The long hot climb made him sweat. The doctor sweated his patient. (V)

Talk   : I have had several talks with him about your problem. (N)
He was talking to a friend. (V)

Tap   : Do not leave the taps running. (N)
It was suspected that he tapped the telephone wires. (V)

Taste   : Sugar has a sweet taste. (N)
If you have a bad cold, you cannot taste anything. It tastes too much of garlic. (V)

Tear   : The sad story moved us to tears. There is a tear in your shirt. (N)
Please tear this sheet of paper into bits. He could not tear himself away from his book (make up his mind to leave). This material tears easily. (V)

Tide   : He was washed up by the tides. You must not ignore the rising tide of public discontent. (N)
He has the ability to tide over this difficulty.

	:	Will Rs. 1000 tide you over until you get your wages? (V)
Time	:	The world exists in space and time. I have no time for sport. (N)
		He timed his journey so that he arrived before dark. (V)
Tip	:	The bird measured 12 inches from tip to tip. (N)
		He tipped the table up. (V)
Toll	:	The war took a heavy toll of the nation's manhood (N).
		The funeral bell tolled solemnly. (V)
Tone	:	He spoke in an angry tone. (N)
		The excitement toned down. (V)
Top	:	Write your name at the top of the page. He came out at the top of the list. (N)
		He topped the list of successful candidates. When we topped the hill we had a fine view. (V)
Touch	:	Even the slightest touch will break a soap-bubble. (N)
		He touched the feet of his Guru. (V)
Trace	:	The police were unable to find any trace of the thief. We have lost all trace of them. (N)
		He traced the words laboriously. The rumour was traced back to a journalist. (V)
Transfer	:	He applied for a transfer to the government. (N)
		The head office has been transferred from Cuttack to Bhubaneswar. The dog has transferred its affection to its new master. (V)
Transport	:	My car is being repaired so I am without transport. (N)
		On hearing of the victory, the nation was transported with joy. (V)
Trick	:	He got the money from you by a trick. He knows all the tricks of the trade. (N)
		He tricked the poor girl out of her money. (V)
Trouble	:	Her heart was full of trouble. His troubles are over now. (N)
		Do not trouble to meet him at the statio. was troubled by the bad news. (V)
Turn	:	The tide is on the turn. He was fr. every turn. (N)

		The earth turns round the sun. He turned his head and looked back. (V)
Twist	:	Give the rope a few more twists. There are numerous twists in the road over the pass. (N) His features were twisted with pain. (V)
Use	:	You must make good use of any opportunities to practise English. (N) When persuasion failed they used force. (V)
Vault	:	He kept his jewels in the vault at the bank. (N) The jockey vaulted into the saddle. (V)
Verge	:	He is on the verge of death. The country is on the verge of disaster. (N) The sun was verging towards the horizon. Such ideas verged on foolhardiness. (V)
View	:	The speaker stood in full view of the crowd. As we rounded the bend we came in view of the lake. (N) The subject may be viewed in various ways. (V)
Visit	:	He went on a visit to the seaside. (N) His rich relations seldom visit him. (V)
Voice	:	He is not in good voice. He has lost his voice. I did not recognise his voice. (N) The spokesman voiced the feelings of the crowd. (V)
Volunteer	:	He is known as a good volunteer. (N) He volunteered some information. How many of them volunteered? (V)
Vow	:	He has taken a vow to take revenge upon his enemy. (N) He vowed to avenge the insult. (V)
Water	:	Blood is thicker than water. (N) He waters the plants with his own hands. (V)
		They gave us a warm welcome. (N) He is welcome to use the public library. (V)
		We heard the whistle of a steam-engine. (N) The engine whistled before reaching the level-crossing. (V)
		He has got wind of the secret. He ran like the wind. (N) The hound winded the fox. The deer winded the stalkers. (V)

Words Used Both as Nouns and as Verbs

Winter	:	These vegetables are available in winter. (N), The regiment wintered in Burma. (V)
Wonder	:	They were filled with wonder. (N) Can you wonder at it? (V)
Word	:	When we speak, we put our thoughts into words. (N) The application has not been properly worded. (V)
Work	:	Are you fond of hard work? This is the work of an enemy. (N) Our statesmen worked hard for peace. The men in this factory work 40 hours a week. (V)
Wound	:	The dog was licking its wounds. (N) Ten soldiers were killed and thirty wounded. (V)
Wrench	:	He gave his ankle a wrench. (N) She wrenched herself from the villain's clutches. (V)
Wrinkle	:	He is beginning to get wrinkles round his eyes. (N) The front of this dress wrinkles. (V)
Yell	:	They greeted him with yells of hate. (N) They yelled with fright. (V)
Yield	:	What is the yield per acre? The yields on his shares have increased this year. (N) They will yield only to force. He yielded to the temptation. (V)
Yoke	:	You have three yokes of oxen. (N) He yoked the oxen together. (V)

EXERCISE

Make sentences of your own, using the following words first as Nouns and then as Verbs:

Accord, age, arrest, alarm, appeal, bias, bitter, blast, boast, build, bother, chair, chance, care, charm, colour, delight, doubt, esteem, eye, fatigue, foil, guard, house, last, judge, iron, measure, man, nod, motion, occasion, pain, paint, pride, roll, say, shade, strain, stain, time, tide, sweat, vault, vow, water, welcome, wonder.

7
WORDS USED WITH APPROPRIATE PREPOSITIONS

Certain Verbs, Nouns, Adjectives and Participles are usually followed by certain Prepositions. All that is required of a learner is that he must make the correct use of the Preposition after certain words. Since there are no definite rules to guide him properly in his use of Prepositions after Verbs, Nouns, Adjectives and Participles, the learner has to develop the habit of reading and using them time and again. Besides, his experience in reading will be of immense help. The following is a list of words used with Prepositions:

A) *Verbs followed by Prepositions:*

Abide by	: You must abide by the rules and regulations of the college. You will have to abide by the consequences.
Abound in, with	: The river abounds in fish. The hut abounded with vermin.
Abstain from	: He should abstain from alcoholic drinks. The doctor advised him to abstain from beer and wine.
Accede to	: The prince acceded to the throne. You should willingly accede to his proposal. He acceded to a political party.
Account for	: He has been asked to account for his conduct. His illness accounts for his absence.
Accuse of	: He accused them of theft. He was accused of bribery.
Acquit of	: He was acquitted of the crime. The judge acquitted him of murder.

Agree to, with	:	Shilpa's father has agreed to her marrying Bibhuti. He agreed to my proposal. The climate does not agree with me. The verb agrees with its subject in number and person.
Aim at	:	He aimed (his gun) at the tiger. My remarks were not aimed at you.
Answer to, for	:	The dog answers to the name of Mitty. He does not answer to the description of the missing man that appeared in the newspapers. I cannot answer for his honesty. I will answer for it (promise) that the next one will be better.
Apologise to, for	:	I apologised to him for my mistake. The girl apologised for her rudeness.
Appeal to, for	:	The prisoner appealed to the judge for mercy. He appealed to the rich man for monetary help.
Apply to, for	:	He applied to the consul for a visa. He applied to the government for medical leave.
Appear in, at, before:		These boys appeared in (at) the examination. The defendant failed to appear before the court.
Approve of	:	Her father will never approve of her marriage with you. I do not approve of your conduct.
Argue with	:	He argued with them about that matter. They argued with me against the proposal.
Arrive at, in	:	They arrived at Shimla. He arrived at the conclusion. At last they arrived in the harbour.
Ask for, after, from :		He asked me for help. He asked after you. He asked for assistance from his neighbours.
Aspire after, to	:	He aspires after knowledge. He aspires to fame. He aspires to become an author.
Associate with	:	Naresh associated himself with Manish in a business undertaking. We associate

	Egypt with the Nile. Do not associate with dishonest boys.
Assure of	: He assured me of his readiness to help.
Attack with, by	: He was attacked with mild fever. They were attacked by the hooligans.
Attend to, upon,	: He attends to the wants of customers. He with sincerity attends to his work. He attended upon the patient. Our plans were attended with great difficulties.
Avail of, on, against	: You should avail yourself of every opportunity to practise speaking English. Money does not avail on a desert island. Nothing availed against the storm.
Beg of, for	: I beg of you not to take any risks. I begged of him to stay. He was so poor that he had to beg for his bread.
Believe in	: I believe in that man. He believes in getting plenty of exercise. He believes in old-fashioned remedies.
Begin at, with, upon	: Today we begin at page 30, line 12. He began with the first topic. Let's begin upon our task now.
Belong to	: These books belong to me. Which club do you belong to?
Bestow on	: He got into the train and bestowed his luggage on the rack. The king bestowed high honours on him. They bestowed praise upon him.
Beware of	: You must beware of pickpockets. You must beware of that dangerous man.
Bind to	: Joan of Arc was bound to the stake and burnt to death. His dog was bound to a tree with a rope.
Blessed with	: I am not greatly blessed with worldly goods. May you always be blessed with good health.
Blind to	: Mothers are sometimes blind to the faults of their children.

Blush for, with, at	:	She blushed for (with) shame. She blushed at her own faults. He blushed for you.
Bound on, by, to, with	:	England is bounded on the north by Scotland. You should bound your desires to what is reasonable. You should bound your desires by reason. His heart bounded with joy.
Bristle with	:	The problem bristles with difficulties.
Burst into, in	:	The oil-stove upset and burst into flames. She suddenly burst into tears. They burst the door in.
Busy about, with	:	He busied himself with (about) all sorts of little tasks.
Care for	:	He does not care for your opinion.
Caution against	:	Please caution him against the danger that he is facing.
Change into	:	He changed into his working clothes.
Charge with, at, for	:	He was charged with the task of keeping the club's accounts in order. He charged them with neglecting their duties. The wounded tiger suddenly charged at him. How much do you charge for mending a pair of shoes?
Close in, with	:	The days are closing in. Darkness closed in on us. I closed with (accepted) the offer.
Clothe in, with	:	The woman was clothed in her finest dress. He clothed his thoughts with (in) words. He was clothed with shame.
Commend to	:	This book does not commend itself to the public.
Commence on, with	:	The examination will commence on Wednesday with mathematics. The proceedings commenced with a song.
Comment on (upon)	:	He commented on his behaviour.
Commit to	:	Commit this paragraph to memory.
Communicate with, to	:	We can communicate with people in most parts of the world by telephone. I communicate with him regularly by letter. Please communicate this message to my friend.

Compare with, to	:	This cannot compare with that. He cannot compare with Shakespeare as a writer of tragedies. Let's compare my notes with yours. Mine cannot be compared to yours. Poets have compared sleep to death. Genius is sometimes compared to a lightning flash.
Compete with, for	:	Many boys competed with him for the prize.
Complain of, against, to	:	The teacher complained of the boy's behaviour to the headmaster. They complained against him to the director.
Comply with	:	He did not comply with my request. I willingly complied with his request.
Concerned with, about, for	:	He is not concerned with this matter. Please do not be concerned about me. We are all concerned for her safety.
Conceal from	:	He concealed all these facts from his father.
Conceive of	:	Who first conceived the idea of filling bags with gas to make balloons?
Concentrate on (upon)	:	You should concentrate (your attention) on (upon) your work. You will solve the problem if you concentrate upon it.
Concur with, in	:	I concur with him in his decision.
Condemn to	:	We all condemn cruelty to children.
Condole with, in	:	His friends condoled with him in his sorrow.
Confer on	:	The queen conferred knighthoods on several distinguished men. The king conferred high honours on him.
Confide to, in	:	I congratulated him on his success in the examination.
Consent to	:	He didn't consent to my proposal.
Consist of, in	:	A rupee consists of one hundred paise. The managing committee of the college consists of 12 members. The happiness of a country consists in the freedom of its citizens.

Contribute to	:	Drinking alchocal contributed to his ruin. He contributed poems to the monthly magazine for several years. Have you contributed to the poor students' fund?
Convicted of	:	The prisoner was convicted of the crime.
Convince of	:	I am convinced of his honesty. We couldn't convince him of his mistake.
Correspond with, to:		The house exactly corresponds with my needs. His actions do not correspond with his words. His expenses do not correspond to his income. The American Congress corresponds to the British Parliament.
Count on, upon, for,: against		We count on your help. You had better not count upon an increase in your salary this year. Knowledge without common sense counts for little. Such men don't count for anything. He is young and inexperienced, but please do not count that against him.
Deal with, in, out	:	I will deal with this subject later on. These firms deal in Japanese goods. It is the duty of a judge to deal out justice.
Debarred from	:	You are debarred from appearing in the examination.
Decide on	:	He decided on joining the office.
Depend on (upon)	:	Children depend on their parents for food and clothing. Good health depends upon good food, exercise, and getting enough sleep.
Despaired of	:	He despaired of success. His life was despaired of.
Determined on, to	:	He is determined on doing this work today. The athlete was determined to break all the records.
Die of, from	:	He died of cholera. Many people died of plague in Surat. He died from over eating.
Differ from, with	:	French differs from English in having genders for all nouns. I am sorry to differ with you about that question.

Disagree with	:	They all disagreed with him in this matter.
Disapprove of	:	I disapprove of your conduct.
Dispense with	:	He is not yet well enough to dispense with the doctor's services. The new machinery dispenses with manual labour.
Dispose of	:	He doesn't want to dispose of the land. I think we have disposed of all his arguments.
Distinguish between, from	:	People who cannot distinguish between colours are said to be colour-blind. Can you distinguish this colour from that?
Entrust with, to	:	Can I entrust you with the task? Can I entrust this task to you? I will entrust you with the work of supervising the students.
Escape from	:	The thief escaped from the prison. Two of the prisoners have escaped from the prison. The canary has escaped from its cage.
Exchange for, with	:	He exchanged his old car for a new one. Kamalesh exchanged seats with Bimalesh.
Export from	:	Jute is exported from India to England.
Feed on (upon), with	:	Cattle feed chiefly on grass. This moving mechanical device feeds the machine with raw material.
Feel for	:	He feels for the poor man in trouble.
Fill with	:	He filled buckets with water.
Grieve for	:	He still grieves for his dead mother.
Guard against	:	You should guard against disease. You must guard against that bad habit.
Happen to	:	If anything happens to him, let me know. I happened to be out when he called.
Hear of, from, about:		I have never heard of him. I won't hear of such a thing. How often do you hear from your sister? You will hear about this later.
Hide from	:	The future is hidden from us. You shouldn't hide the truth from me.

Hope for, against	:	Let us hope for the best. He has hope against hope.
Import into	:	A lot of machinery is imported into India from abroad.
Impress on (upon), with	:	His words are strongly impressed on my memory. His speech didn't impress upon them the value of discipline. I impressed him with the importance of his work.
Inquire of, for, into	:	I inquired of the servant if his master was at home. He inquired for a book in a shop. We must inquire into the matter.
Insist on (upon)	:	I insist on your being there. The girl insisted on buying a costly dress.
Inspire with	:	His friend inspired him with hope.
Interfere with, in, between	:	Don't interfere with this machine. Do you ever allow pleasure to interfere with duty? Please don't interfere in my business. It's unwise to interfere between husband and wife.
Introduce to, into	:	The teacher introduced the pupils to the intricacies of Euclid. Tobacco was introduced into Europe from America.
Invest in, with	:	He has invested his savings in a business enterprise. The military governor has been invested with full authority.
Invite to	:	He invited his friend to dinner.
Involve in	:	They are deeply involved in debt. Don't involve yourself in unnecessary expenditure.
Irradiate with	:	Their faces were irradiated with joy.
Jest with, in, about	:	He is not a man to jest with. You mustn't jest at a thing which is sacred to others. Don't jest about serious things.
Land at	:	They landed at Bombay.
Listen to	:	Don't listen to him, he wants to get you into trouble. He has always listened to your complaints.
Look at, for, after, about	:	He looked at the picture. We must look at the question from all sides. Will you

please look at this letter? What are you looking for? Who'll look after the children while their mother is in hospital? You should look after your old parents. Are you still looking about for a job? We hardly had time to look about us before we had to continue our journey.

Meet with	:	Yesterday he met with an accident.
Mistake for	:	They mistook him for his brother.
Object to	:	I object to all this noise. I object to him doing that work.
Occur to, in	:	An idea has occurred to me. It didn't occur to me to bring this matter to your notice. These lines occur in the poem *"To a Skylark"*.
Partake of	:	They partook of our simple meal. His manner partakes of insolence.
Part with	:	On that question I am afraid I must part company with you. He hates to part with his money.
Persist in	:	She persists in wearing that old-fashioned necklace.
Prefer to	:	He prefers tea to coffee. He prefers walking to cycling.
Prevent from	:	His father prevented him from making friends with those boys.
Profit by	:	I have profited by your advice.
Prohibit from	:	Tourist-class passengers are prohibited from using the promenade deck.
Protect from	:	May God protect you from harm.
Protest against	:	He protested against being called an old fool.
Provide for, with	:	You should provide for the entertainment of your visitors. He has a large family to provide for. He is already provided with all he needs. He provided them with all kinds of facilities.
Punish for	:	This boy was punished for no fault of his own.

Rebel against	:	The tribes rebelled against the government.
Recover from	:	He is slowly recovering from his illness. Has the country recovered from the effect of the war yet?
Refer to	:	He was referred to the inquiry officer. Don't refer to this matter again, please. Does that remark refer to me?
Refrain from	:	Please refrain from spitting in public places. Let us hope they will refrain from hostile action.
Rejoice at	:	He rejoiced at the success of his brother in the examination.
Relieve of	:	He was relieved of his duties from the office. He was relieved of his post.
Rely on, (upon)	:	You may rely upon my early arrival. You may rely on what I say.
Remind of	:	He reminds me of his brother.
Rescue from	:	The girl rescued her younger brother from drowning.
Rest with, on, against	:	It rests with you to decide. His fame rests upon his plays more than upon his novels. Rest the ladder against the wall.
Restore to	:	Charles II was restored to the throne in 1660.
Result in	:	Their diplomacy resulted in war.
Retire from, to	:	He retired from service. He retired to his cabin. Our soldiers retired to their prepared positions.
Revolt against	:	The people revolted against their rulers.
Reward with	:	The government rewarded him with a medal for his bravery.
Rule over	:	An emperor is a monarch who rules over an empire.
Search for	:	He searched for the missing child everywhere.
Send for	:	Please send for a doctor immediately. Please keep them until I send for them.

Sentence to	:	The Magistrate sentenced the thief to six months' imprisonment.
Smell of	:	The mutton smells disgustingly of garlic.
Start for	:	He started for Germany yesterday.
Struggle against	:	He struggled against many difficulties.
Submit to	:	He submitted himself to discipline. We must submit to God's will.
Subscribe to	:	He subscribed liberally to charities. He subscribed Rs. 100 to the flood relief fund.
Succeed in, to	:	He could succeed in the examination. The prince succeeded to the throne of his uncle.
Supply with	:	The rich man supplied the poor with grain.
Surrender to	:	They advised the bandits to surrender to the police. The proud general didn't surrender to the enemy.
Sympathise with	:	He sympathised with his friend in his afflictions.
Trust in, to, with	:	He has complete trust in God. A child usually has perfect trust in his mother. Don't trust to chance. You have too much trust your memory. You cannot trust your servants with money.
Wait for	:	Wait for me, please. We are waiting for better weather.
Warn of	:	He was warned of the danger.
Wed to	:	He is wedded to his own opinions and nothing can change him.
Yearn for (after)	:	He yearned for (after) a sight of the old, familiar faces.
Yield to	:	The disease yields to treatment. He yielded to the temptation.

B)   *Nouns followed by Prepositions:*

Abhorrence of	:	His abhorrence of flattery is an admirable quality.
In accordance with	:	He acted in accordance with my instructions.

Acquaintance with	:	He has some acquaintance with German but does not speak it fluently.
Admission to, into	:	He could not get admission into a government college. Admission to the Medical college is by entrance examination only.
Advantage of	:	The advantages of good education are great. You should not take advantage of his innocence. He always takes full advantage of the mistakes made by his rivals.
Affection for	:	Every mother has affection for her children.
Anxiety for	:	They waited with anxiety for news of her safe arrival.
Apology for	:	He gave me an apology for his conduct.
Appetite for	:	He has lost his appetite for food.
Application for, to	:	The manager received one hundred applications for the position. They made an application to the court for an inquiry.
Assurance of	:	I have full assurance of his honesty.
Attachment to	:	His attachment to his wife is remarkable.
Attention to	:	Pay attention to what you are doing.
Authority over	:	An officer has authority over the soldiers under him.
Blame for	:	Where does the blame lie for our failure? You mustn't put the blame for the accident upon me.
Care of	:	The library is under the care of Mr. Mohapatra. Take care of your health.
Cause of	:	He is the cause of all the trouble.
Claim to	:	He has no claim to the property.
Comment on (upon):		Have you any comments to make upon my writing?
Compassion	:	His heart was filled with compassion for the refugees. He felt compassion for the poor child.

Complaint against	:	Why don't you lodge a complaint against your noisy neighbours.
Confidence in	:	Don't put too much confidence in what the newspapers say. There is a want of confidence in the government. I hope you will justify my confidence in him.
Connection with	:	He has no connection with them.
Consideration for	:	He has never shown much consideration for his wife's feelings.
Contribution to	:	He has made a contribution to the relief fund.
Control over	:	The teacher has no control over the students.
Delight in	:	The naughty boy takes great delight in pulling the cat's tail.
Demand for	:	There have been demands for the prime minister to resign.
Descent from	:	He traces his descent from a royal family.
Desire for	:	He has no desire for wealth.
Disgrace to, on, with	:	These slums are a disgrace to the municipal authorities. A man who commits a crime and is sent to prison brings disgrace on himself and his family. He has fallen into disgrace with his companions.
Distaste for	:	He has a distaste for hard work.
Doubt about	:	There is not much doubt about his guilt.
Duty to	:	Don't forget your duty to your parents.
Enmity with	:	His enmity with that man is the cause of all his troubles.
Exception to	:	There are certain exceptions to the rules of grammar. He took exception to the statement.
Excuse for	:	He is always making excuses for being late.
Faith in	:	He has an implicit faith in God.
Fondness for	:	He has a great fondness for your family.
Favour of	:	Was he in favour of votes for women?
Grief at	:	He expressed grief at the death of his pet dog.

Hatred for	:	He has hatred for that man.
Heir to	:	He is heir to a large fortune.
Influence over, on, for, of, with	:	They have no influence over that man. Heredity and environment are influences on character. He is an influence for good in the town. He was under the influence of drink. Will you please use your influence with the manager on his behalf?
Inquiry into	:	The authorities held an official inquiry into the matter.
Interest in	:	His two great interests in life are music and painting. He has no interest in politics.
Invitation to	:	They accepted his invitation to dinner.
Leisure for	:	I have no leisure for sport.
Leniency to	:	Your leniency to the boy is the cause of his going astray.
Liking for	:	He developed a great liking for music.
Limit to	:	There is a limit to everything. We must set a limit to the expense of the trip.
Longing for	:	His longing for happiness is the cause of his unhappiness.
Necessity for	:	There was no necessity for asking that question.
Need for, of	:	There's no need for anxiety. He is always in need of money.
Objection to	:	He has a strong objection to getting up early. He took objection to what I said.
Opportunity for	:	The opportunity for the reformers to do this came in 1905.
Opposition to	:	We found ourselves in opposition to our friends on this question.
Passion for	:	He developed a great passion for poetry and music.
Peace with	:	India wants to be at peace with the neighbouring countries.
Pity for	:	His heart is filled with pity for the poor. You should feel pity for the downtrodden.
Precaution against	:	You should take necessary precautions against contagious diseases.

Prejudice against	:	He has a prejudice against modern music.
Preparation for	:	We are getting things together in preparation for the journey.
Pride in	:	He took much pride in the brilliant achievements of his children.
Progress in	:	There is a tremendous progress in civilisation. He made much progress in his studies.
Prohibition against	:	There is prohibition against the use of contaminated water.
Proof of	:	He produced documents in proof of his claim.
Quarrel between	:	The quarrel between the two friends made their enemies laugh at them.
Reason for	:	Give me your reasons for doing it.
Regard for	:	He has very little regard for others.
Regret for	:	They expressed regret for the delay.
Relation between	:	There are friendly relations between India and America. He has business relations with a firm in Stockholm.
Remedy for	:	You should find out a good remedy for the failure of that scheme. Quinine is a remedy for malaria.
Reputation for	:	He has a reputation for displaying courage. He has a great reputation for honesty.
Share of, in	:	You must take your share of the blame. You are not taking much share in the conversation.
Slave to	:	He is a slave to drink.
Surety for	:	He stood surety for the accused.
Taste for, in, of	:	He has a taste for Manila cigars. She has excellent taste in dress. Won't you have a taste of this cake?
Traitor to	:	He was a traitor to his country.
Trust in	:	He hasn't much trust in your promises.
Victim of	:	A fund was opened to help the victims of the earthquake. Many people were victims of the plague in Surat.

Victory over	:	They gained a victory over their enemies.
Volley of	:	They went on asking a volley of questions to their leader.
Wait for	:	We had a long wait for the bus.
Want of	:	The earthquake victims are suffering from a want of medical supplies.
Yell of	:	They greeted us with a yell of hate.
Yield of	:	There is a good yield of wheat this year.
Zeal for	:	He shows great zeal for sports and games.

C) *Adjectives and Participles followed by Prepositions:*

Absorbed in	:	They found him absorbed in studies.
Acceptable to	:	His proposal is not acceptable to us.
Accountable for, to	:	A madman is not accountable for his actions. You are accountable to me for this money.
Accustomed to	:	His father is not accustomed to this kind of life.
Accessory to	:	The servant was an accessory to the crime.
Acquainted with	:	He is not fully acquainted with the case.
Active in	:	He is active in doing good to others.
Accomplished in	:	He is accomplished in painting.
Addicted to	:	He is addicted to gambling.
Adapted to	:	Camels are usually adapted to life in the desert.
Adequate to	:	The sum of Rs 100 a week is not adequate to support a family.
Affectionate to	:	He was very affectionate to me.
Afraid of	:	I am afraid of hurting his feelings.
Agreeable to	:	Are you agreeable to the proposal?
Alarmed at	:	They became alarmed at the rumour.
Alien to	:	Cruelty was quite alien to his nature.
Alternative to	:	There are alternative answers to that problem.
Amaze at	:	I was amazed at the news.
Amused at	:	The children were amused at the story-teller's jokes.

Angry at, with	:	He was angry at being kept waiting. He was angry with himself for having made such a foolish mistake.
Annoyed with	:	He got annoyed with him for his careless work.
Answerable to	:	He is answerable to the principal in office matters. You are answerable to him for your conduct.
Antipathetic	:	He is antipathetic to their attitudes.
Anxious about, for	:	I am very anxious about my son's health. He is anxious for her safety.
Apologetic for	:	He was apologetic for arriving late.
Applicable to	:	Is the rule applicable to this case?
Appropriate to, for	:	Write in a style appropriate to your subject. Thick woollen clothes are not appropriate for a hot summer day.
Apprehensive of, for:		They are apprehensive of further defeats. He is apprehensive for her safety.
Approximate to	:	He took a sum of money approximate to what will be needed.
Ashamed of	:	He is ashamed of cheating.
Astonished at	:	They are astonished at his rudeness.
Aware of	:	We are fully aware of the gravity of the situation.
Backward in	:	Soumendra is backward in his studies because of his long illness. Although he is clever, he is backward in giving his views.
Beneficial to	:	Fresh air and good food are beneficial to the health.
Bent on	:	He is bent on creating a disturbance during the Annual Cultural Function of the college.
Beset with	:	The path of a reformer is beset with difficulties.
Blind of, to, in	:	He is blind of one eye. Mothers are sometimes blind to the faults of their children. He is blind in the right eye.

Born of	:	Subhendu is born of rich parents.
Blue with	:	His face was blue with cold.
Bound for	:	The ship is bound for Finland.
Brave of	:	It was brave of him to enter the burning building.
Busy with	:	He was busy with his work.
Capable of	:	He is capable of any crime. The situation is capable of improvement. Show your teacher what you are capable of.
Careful about, of, with	:	She is careful about her dress. Be careful of your health. Be more careful with your work.
Charged with	:	He was charged with an important mission.
Close to	:	The post office is close to his house.
Competent for	:	Is he competent for this kind of work?
Composed of	:	Water is composed of hydrogen and oxygen.
Condemned to	:	The murderer was condemned to death.
Confident of	:	He is confident of his own success.
Conscious of	:	They are conscious of being watched. He was conscious of his guilt.
Content with	:	Are you content with your present salary? She is content with very little.
Contented with	:	He is contented with his lot.
Contrary to	:	The result was contrary to expectation.
Convicted of	:	The accused was convicted of the crime.
Convinced of	:	He is quite convinced of your simplicity.
Courteous to	:	Dinesh is courteous to all.
Cured of	:	He is cured of his disease.
Deaf to, of	:	He turned a deaf ear to their requests for help. He is deaf of one ear.
Delighted with	:	He was delighted with his brother's success.
Dependent on (upon)	:	The man was out of work and dependent upon his son's earnings. Promotion is dependent upon your record of success.
Deprived of	:	They were deprived of victory for want of time.

Desirous of	:	He is desirous of winning a prize. He is desirous of peace.
Determined on	:	He is determined on becoming a social worker.
Different from	:	Your method is different from mine.
Diffident about	:	He is diffident about achieving success in the examination.
Disappointed in, with	:	He is disappointed in his brother's results. He is disappointed with you.
Disgusted with	:	The teacher is disgusted with the pupil's conduct.
Eager for, about	:	Who is not eager for fame? He is eager about his progress. She is eager for achieving success.
Engaged in	:	He is engaged in difficult work.
Entitled to	:	The officer is entitled to house rent as admissible by government rules.
Essential to, for	:	Is wealth essential to happiness? Exercise, fresh air, and sleep are essential for the preservation of health.
Exempted from	:	He was exempted from the payment of the monthly tuition fee to the college.
Exposed to	:	He was exposed to danger on the roads.
Faithful to	:	He is faithful to his promise. The dog is faithful to its master.
Familiar with	:	He is not very familiar with botanical names.
Famous for	:	Puri is famous for Lord Jagannath's Temple.
Fit for	:	That man is not fit for the position. It was a dinner fit for a king.
Fond of	:	She is very fond of music.
Free from	:	You are free from blame in this affair.
Full of	:	The room was full of people.
Good for	:	Milk is good for children. He is good for nothing.
Grateful to, for	:	We are grateful to you for your help.
Greedy for	:	That businessman is greedy for gain.
Guilty of	:	He was found guilty of murder.
Honest in	:	He is honest in all his dealings.

Hopeful of, about	:	He is hopeful of his success in the examination. Shyamananda is hopeful about his future.
Horrified at	:	They were horrified at the murder.
Ignorant of	:	You are not ignorant of the reasons for his behaviour.
Ill with	:	She was ill with anxiety.
Indifferent to	:	The explorers were indifferent to the discomforts and dangers of the expedition.
Indebted to	:	He is indebted to you for your help.
Independent of	:	If you have a motorcar, you are independent of trains and buses.
Indulgent to	:	Generally parents are indulgent to their children.
Infested with	:	His house is infested with rats.
Injurious to	:	Smoking is injurious to health.
Inspired with	:	They were all inspired with hope after his speech.
Intent on	:	He is intent on mischief.
Interested in	:	He is not interested in mathematics.
Intimate with	:	Subhas is intimate with Ramanendra.
Involved in	:	Why are you involved in such nefarious activity?
Jealous of	:	He is jealous of your success.
Lavish in	:	The rich man is lavish in his expenditure.
Liable to	:	If you drive a car dangerously you make yourself liable to a heavy fine, or even to imprisonment.
Loyal to	:	We must remain loyal to the government.
Made of	:	The temple is made of stone.
Married to	:	She is married to her cousin.
Mistaken for	:	You were mistaken for his brother.
Moved by	:	They were moved by his speech.
Necessary to	:	Sleep is necessary to health.
Negligent in	:	He was negligent in his work.
Obedient to	:	The boys are obedient to their teachers.
Obliged to	:	He is obliged to you for your help.
Offended with	:	She was offended with her husband.

Opposed to	:	I am very opposed to your going abroad.
Partial to	:	There are some examiners who are partial to pretty women students.
Peculiar to	:	This is a custom peculiar to the Hindus.
Popular with	:	He is popular with his neighbours.
Proper for	:	This is not a proper time for merry-making. Your dress is proper for this occasion.
Polite in	:	Ardhendu is polite in his behaviour.
Preferable to	:	I find coffee preferable to tea.
Prepared for	:	These boys are not fully prepared for the examination.
Proud of	:	He is proud of his family background.
Qualified for	:	You are not fully qualified for teaching music.
Quick at	:	He is very quick at figures.
Ready for	:	The troops are ready for action.
Reduced to	:	His family was reduced to poverty.
Related to	:	Are you related to Mr. Das?
Relevant to	:	You must supply the facts relevant to the case.
Respectful to	:	He is respectful to his higher authorities.
Responsible to	:	You are responsible to the manager for the petty cash.
Satisfied with	:	He is not quite satisfied with his position.
Sensitive to	:	The eyes are sensitive to light.
Serviceable to	:	Your warm coat will be serviceable in winter.
Shocked at	:	They are all shocked at your behaviour.
Short of	:	Are you short of money? The car broke down when we were still five miles short of our destination.
Sick of, for	:	He was sick of a fever. He is sick of the whole business. He has been sick for six weeks.
Similar to, in	:	Gita's necklace is similar to Rita's. Gold is similar in colour to brass. My wife and I have similar interests in gardening.
Sorry for, about	:	I should be sorry for you to think that I

	dislike you. Aren't you sorry for (about) what you have done?
Subordinate to	: The lecturers are subordinate to the principal.
Sufficient for	: Have you sufficient food for 10 people? Is Rs. 5000 sufficient for the expenses of your journey?
Suited to	: You should live in a style suited to your conditions.
Sure of	: Can we be sure of his honesty? You are sure of a welcome.
Suspicious of, to	: He is suspicious of everybody. The affair looks suspicious to me.
Thankful to, for	: They should be thankful to you for your help. Be thankful for small mercies.
Tired of	: They are tired of arguing with him.
True to	: You should be true to your words. Plants grown from seed are not always true to type.
Useful for, to	: The coconut tree is useful for many purposes. This book is useful to me.
Unfit for	: He is unfit for business. This road is unfit for heavy traffic.
Versed in	: He is well-versed in painting.
Vested in	: All the powers are vested in the secretary.
Visible to	: The eclipse will be visible to observers in Western Europe.
Void of	: His proposal is void of reason.
Vulnerable to	: Are you vulnerable to ridicule?
Wanting in	: He is wanting in courtesy.
Weak in	: That boy is weak in English.
Worthy of	: His behaviour is worthy of praise.

D) Sometimes it is found that a word that takes a certain Preposition after it in one context, uses a different Preposition in another context; as,

He *confided* his troubles *to* his friend.
There is no one here I can *confide in*.
I don't much *care about* going.
He doesn't much *care for* television.

He *beguilded* me *into* lending him most of my savings.

Our journey was *beguiled with* pleasant talk.

You should *avail* yourself *of* this opportunity.

Money doesn't *avail on* a desert island.

Nothing *availed against* the storm.

I am very *anxious about* my son's health. He is *anxious* for his daughter's safety.

We must *look at* the question from all sides. The nurse *looks after* his children. He is *looking for* a job.

He has a good *command of* the English language.

He has no *command over* himself.

There are certain Verbs which sometimes take Prepositions after them, but sometimes do not take any at all. In both cases the meaning becomes different and is not always the same.

The collector *conducted* the interview.

The servant conducted him *in*.

He *attends* his classes regularly.

He *attends to* what I am saying.

He *dispensed* charity *to* people.

The new machinery *dispenses with* manual labour.

Don't forget to *count* your change. We *count upon* your help.

He *dwelt* in a slum area. He *dwells* too much *upon* his past.

If you shut your eyes, you can't *see*.

The solicitors will *see into* your claim to the property.

The police *searched* the criminal to see what he had in his pocket.

He *searched* all his drawers *for* the missing papers.

We write regularly but seldom *meet*.

He *met with* an accident yesterday.

There are certain words which take Prepositions immediately after them. In such cases, the Preposition placed after the word must be followed not by an Infinitive but by a Gerund.

The following sentences illustrate this point:

He is accustomed to doing it (not 'to do').

He is addicted to drinking (not 'to drink').

He believes in getting plenty of exercise.

Manas aims at becoming a doctor in life.

Abanikant is confident of winning the prize.

He is bent on doing this work.

Mr. Das is qualified for holding the post of managing director of the Corporation.

He is fond of eating bread.

He is an expert in fabricating statements.

He is desirous of going abroad.

Rakesh has no chance of getting a first class in the examination.

He insisted upon finishing the work.

The boy was assured of getting a seat in the science stream of the college.

She was greatly interested in learning music.

Similarly there are certain words which always take the Infinitive after them. No Preposition is used before an Infinitive or a Clause. The following examples illustrate this point:

He asked him to do some work.

I am inclined to think that he is opposed to the plan.

He declined to discuss his plans.

Nirmal hoped to get the prize.

He will be interested to know what happens.

He intends to apply for the higher post.

We were pleased to hear that he had recovered from his illness.

We were glad to be home again.

He was very careful to see that everything was locked up before he left the office.

The old lady was afraid to cross the road.

Be careful to lock the safe.

Be careful not to spill the liquid.

We are sorry to hear that you have not been well.

I am sorry to say that he didn't keep his word.

Take care to lock everything up safely.

We were pleased that you have been able to come.

Note: When certain words are followed by infinitives, no preposition is used. Such words as are used in the above sentences do not take prepositions when followed by an infinitive. Besides, no preposition is used before a clause.

E)   *Related Words followed by Different Prepositions.*
     Below are some of the related words which take different
     Prepositions after them.

Abhorrence of	:	His abhorrence of flattery is praiseworthy.
Abhorrent to	:	Cruelty to animals is abhorrent to us.
According to	:	He acted according to your advice.
Accordance with	:	That book is written strictly in accordance with the prescribed syllabus of the University.
Affection for	:	His affection for his younger brother is very great.
Affectionate to	:	The teacher is affectionate to his pupils.
Alien to	:	Cruelty was quite alien to his nature.
Alienated from	:	Shovan was alienated from his friends.
Alternate with	:	He alternated kindness with severity.
Alternative to	:	Is there no alternative to what you propose?
Ambition for	:	Gopal has a great ambition for fame.
Ambitious of	:	He is ambitious of achieving fame.
Avail of	:	He availed himself of casual leave for five days.
Available for	:	These tickets are available for one month.
Capable of	:	He is capable of winning her heart.
Capacity for	:	He has no capacity for business.
Confidence in	:	I have no confidence in him.
Confident of	:	He is confident of his success in the examination.
Contrast to	:	His white hair was in sharp contrast to his dark skin.
Contrast between	:	The contrast between the two brothers is remarkable.
Contrast with	:	Subhendu's marks are excellent in contrast with Kailash's marks.
Delight in	:	The queen delights in music.
Delighted at	:	He was delighted at the sight of the daffodil flowers.
Descended from	:	He is descended from a noble family.
Descendant of	:	He is a descendant of the Nizam of

	Hyderabad.
Desire for	: He has a great desire for fame.
Desirous of	: Ramanendra's father is desirous of visiting Gaya.
Equal to	: He was equal to the occasion.
Equally with	: He is to be equally blamed with his brother.
Exception to	: It is an exception to the general rule.
Excepted from	: The thief was excepted from punishment.
Excluded from	: His name was excluded from the list of volunteers.
Exclusive of	: The ship had a crew of 60, exclusive of officers.
Favourable to, for	: His reply is not favourable to you. The time is not favourable for your action.
Favoured with	: He was favoured with a reply.
Filled with	: I was filled with admiration.
Fond of	: She is very fond of music.
Fondness for	: He has a great fondness for his children.
Founded on	: His arguments are founded on facts.
Foundation in	: This story has no foundation in fact.
Full of	: His heart was full of joy.
Hindered from	: He hindered them from going.
Hindrance to	: Certain customs are a great hindrance to social progress.
Included in	: This item is included in the list.
Inclusive of	: This is the price of the book inclusive of postal charges.
Indulge in	: He indulged in bad habits.
Indulgent to	: No father should be indulgent to his children.
Liking for	: He has a great liking for cricket.
Dislike of	: My dislike of him continued to increase.
Neglectful of	: He is neglectful of his own interest.
Negligent in	: He was negligent in his work.
Partial to	: They say he is partial to his friends.
Partiality for	: He has a great partiality for men of his own caste and religion.
Qualified for	: You are really qualified for that post.

Disqualified from	:	You are disqualified from practising as a lawyer.
Result or	:	As result of an injury, he died in the hospital.
Respect for	:	They have great respect for his knowledge of English.
Resulted from	:	No decision resulted from the conference.
Respectful to	:	He is respectful to his authorities.
Satisfactory to	:	His conduct is not satisfactory to his teacher.
Satisfied with	:	Are you satisfied with your income?
Seized upon	:	He seized upon the opportunity offered to him.
Seizure of	:	The seizure of his property was carried out under direct orders from the District Magistrate.
Sensible of	:	That was sensible of you. He is sensible of the danger of his position.
Sensitive to	:	Children are usually sensitive to blame.
Sure of	:	He is sure of his success.
Surety for	:	He stood surety for his friend.
Trust in	:	His trust in God is great.
Distrust of	:	His distrust of you is very great.
Want of	:	Your work shows want of thought.
Wanting in	:	Our people are wanting in courage.

EXERCISES

1. Fill in the blanks with appropriate Prepositions in the following sentences:
   a) He certainly differs _____ you in this matter.
   b) There are some people in the country who are not at all in favour _____ granting freedom to women.
   c) The demand _____ patent medicine is unfortunately growing.
   d) I am indifferent alike _____ praise and blame.
   e) Death does not distinguish _____ the rich and poor.
   f) He has no interest _____ literature.

Idioms/Phrases		Usage
Adam's apple	-	*Part that sticks out in the front of the throat and moves up and down when one speaks.* We cannot know a man from his Adam's apple.
After all	-	*Nevertheless, on the whole.* He is a kind-hearted man after all.
After a man's own soul or heart	-	*Exactly what one likes or admires.* He is a man after my own heart.
An afternoon farmer	-	*One who loses the best time for work, lazy.* Bikash is too much of an afternoon farmer to carry on his business successfully.
Against a rainy day	-	*For a time of possible need.* You should save money against a rainy day.
Agreeably to	-	*In accordance with.* Agreeably to your instruction, he did the work satisfactorily.
All along	-	*For the whole length of; all the time; from the start.* There are trees all along the road. I have all along made you aware of that problem.
All at once	-	*Suddenly.* The stranger attacked him all at once.
All in all	-	*Of supreme or exclusive importance, interest, etc.* They were all in all to each other.
All one	-	*All the same.* Do as you like, it is all one to me.
All the same	-	*Nevertheless.* It is all the same to me whether you do it or not. He scolded him for his idleness but encouraged him all the same.
All and sundry	-	*Everyone without distinction.* He invited all and sundry to attend the meeting. The government granted financial benefits to all and sundry.
All the while	-	*During the whole period.* He was all the while talking about those matters.

Idioms/Phrases	Usage
Along of	- *Owing to; because of.* It is all along of you that he could succeed in his examination.
Along with	- *Together.* He went to the market along with his sister.
Animal spirits	- *The liveliness that comes from health and physical exhilaration.* She had high animal spirits.
Anything but	- *Not at all.* His conduct is anything but agreeable.
Apple of one's eye	- *A much prized treasure.* He kept him as the apple of his eye.
Apple of discord	- *Something which causes strife.* The letter was his long contemplated apple of discord.
Apple - pie order	- *Extreme neatness.* The children's garden is in apple-pie order.
Arm in arm	- *Walking in a friendly fashion with arms linked.* They were walking upto the garden together arm in arm.
At arm's length	- *At a certain distance; avoiding too great nearness or familiarity.* He kept them at arm's length.
As a matter of fact	- *In reality.* As a matter of fact, they did not lend their support to him.
As a rule	- *Usually.* As a rule, he goes to the college at 10.30 a.m. everyday.
As to	- *With regard to.* We know nothing as to that matter.
As if	- *As one would (if).* He behaved as if he knew nothing about that matter.
As ill luck would have it	- *Unfortunately.* As ill luck would have it, he could not succeed in the examination.
As in duty bound	- We shall, as in duty bound, ever pray for your long life and prosperity.
As it were	- *So to speak.* He was, as it were, a kind-hearted man.
At a loss	- *Puzzled.* He is at a loss to take any decision.

Idioms/Phrases	Usage
At a stretch	- *Without stopping to rest.* He can write twenty pages at a stretch.
At all events	- *Whatever may happen.* At all events, you must do your work.
At all cost	- They decided to continue the agitation at all cost.
At daggers drawn	- *In a state of hostility.* He is at daggers drawn with his brother.
At home in	- *Familiar.* He is at home in physics.
At issue	- *In dispute.* That was the point at issue.
At length	- *In the end, in full.* The criminal was at length arrested by the police. You are required to write your name at length.
At one	- *In agreement.* I am at one with you in this regard.
At one's beck and call	- *Under one's complete control.* His servant is at his beck and call.
At one's elbow	- *Close beside one.* He would have his friend always at his elbow.
At one's sweet will	- *At pleasure.* He did his work at his sweet will.
At random	- *Without any precision or purpose.* He went on talking at random.
At sixes and sevens	- *In disorder.* The boy left all his books on the floor of the room at sixes and sevens.
At stake	- *In danger.* His life is at stake.
At the eleventh hour	- *Last moment.* He revealed the secret at the eleventh hour of his life.
At the instance of	- *At the direction of.* This thing was done at the instance of his brother.
At variance with	- *Different from.* His action is at variance with his words.
Bad debts	- *Debts of which there is no hope that they will ever be paid.* Among his assets he had included a number of bad debts.
Bag and baggage	- *With all one's belongings.* He left the place, bag and baggage.
Beau ideal	- *Highest conceivable type.* His ambition is to give them a beau ideal welcome.

Idioms/Phrases	Usage
Beauty is but skin-deep	- *Beauty is a thing which can be easily destroyed, and should not, therefore, be valued too highly.* Marry a woman for her good qualities; beauty is but skin-deep.
Because of	- *On account of; by reason of.* Because of his bad leg, he could not walk as fast as the others.
Bed of roses	- *A pleasant and easy condition of life.* The post of a prime minister is not a bed of roses.
Behind one's back	- *Without one's knowledge or consent.* I do not want to listen to what you say about the man behind his back.
Behind time	- *Late.* The train arrived half an hour behind time.
Behind the times	- *Not abreast of changes.* This writer is behind the times.
Below the mark	- *Less than the required standard.* Your performance is below the mark.
Beside the mark	- *Having nothing to do with.* Your remarks are not beside the mark.
Between Scylla and Charybdis	- *Between two menacing dangers; avoiding one, you fall into the other.* You have your Scylla and your Charybdis, as pastor of the congregation; if you preach the old theology, you will lose the young men and if you preach the new, you will alienate the old men.
Between you and me	- *In confidence.* Between them they soon finished the work.
Bubble and squeak	- *Used contemptuously of what is little prized.* All his talk of rank and title is bubble and squeak!
Buridan's ass	- *A man of indecision.* He was a buridan's ass of a man and seldom came to a decision till it was too late.
Beside one's self	- *Out of one's senses.* Nirmal was beside himself with joy to hear of his success in the examination.

Idioms/Phrases	Usage
Beyond all question	- *Without any doubt.* It is beyond all question that Lal Bahadur Shastri was a friend of the poor and the needy.
Black and blue	- The teacher beat the boy black and blue. (so as to bring out black and blue marks on the skin)
Bona fide	- *Genuine.* Are you a bonafide student of this college?
Burning question	- *A question of general concern or that causes excitement.* What is the burning question of the day in our country? Scams are the burning questions of the day.
By all means	- *Certainly; at all costs.* He will do this work by all means.
By degrees	- *Gradually.* Their friendship by degrees grew into love.
By dint of	- *By force of.* He achieved success by dint of hard labour.
By the by	- *In passing.* By the by, did you send that message to your friend?
By the way	- *Incidentally.* By the way, he asked them this question.
By halves	- *Partially.* You should not do your work by halves.
By leaps and bounds	- *Very rapidly.* Prices of all essential commodities increased by leaps and bounds.
By fits and starts	- *In short periods, from time to time, not regularly.* You cannot succeed in the examination if you read by fits and starts.
By hook or by crook	- *By any means; by one means or another.* You have to do that work by hook or by crook.
By virtue of	- *Because of.* He claimed a pension by virtue of his long military service.
Far from	- *Very different.* Your work is far from being satisfactory. The newspaper accounts are far from being true.
Few and far between	- *Not many in number.* His visits there are few and far between.

Idioms/Phrases		Usage
Flesh and blood	-	*Human nature with its emotions, weakness, etc.* Flesh and blood cannot bear such insults silently.
Crocodile tears	-	*Affected tears.* She is shedding merely crocodile tears.
Dog-in-the manger policy	-	*Not allowing other men to follow what one does not like.* He is following a dog-in-the-manger policy.
Fish out of water	-	*Feeling helpless.* He feels like a fish out of water.
Fish in troubled waters	-	*Try to win advantages for oneself from a disturbed state of affairs.* It is his nature to fish in troubled waters.
For all the world	-	*For any consideration whatever.* She is unwilling to part with that ring for all the world.
For good	-	*Permanently.* He will shift to that house for good.
For the sake of	-	He is prepared to do anything for the sake of friendship.
From A to Z	-	*Completely or fully.* What he says about this matter is right from A to Z.
From hand to mouth	-	*With difficulty.* They managed to live their lives from hand to mouth.
From the bottom of one's heart	-	*Heartily.* He likes him from the bottom of his heart.
Hairbreadth escape	-	*A narrow escape.* While swimming in the river he was carried away by the current, but he had a hairbreadth escape.
Hard and fast	-	*Fixed, that cannot be altered to fit special cases.* There is no hard and fast rule in this matter.
Heart and soul	-	*Earnestly.* He did his work heart and soul.
Head and shoulders	-	*Very much.* Tennyson was head and shoulders above other poets of his age.
Hole and corner	-	*Secret.* They do not appreciate a hole and corner policy.
In a fix	-	*In a dilemma, awkward or difficult situation.* He is in a fix and is unable to decide what to do.

Idioms/Phrases	Usage
In a nutshell	- *Briefly.* He explained the matter in a nutshell.
In abeyance	- *In a state of suspension.* His transfer was kept in abeyance.
In accordance	: *According to.* This book is written in accordance with the prescribed syllabus of the University.
Inasmuch as	- *Since.* You deserve punishment inasmuch as you have been proved guilty.
In black and white	- *In writing.* You should put forth your grievances in black and white.
In cold blood	- *Without provocation.* He was put to death in cold blood.
In fine	- *In conclusion.* In fine, the magistrate set the criminal free.
In force	- *In effect, valid.* These rules are no longer in force.
In good part	- *Without getting offended.* They took his jokes in good part.
In keeping with	- *In harmony with.* Your manners are not in keeping with your status.
In one's element	- *In suitable or satisfying surroundings.* He is in his element when taking part in a political debate.
In prospect of	- *With the future in mind.* He studied science with mathematics as one of his optional subjects in prospect of joining the Engineering college.
In pursuance of	- *In fulfilment of.* He is prepared to do anything in pursuance of his object.
In quest of	- *Search or pursuit, seeking for.* He went off in quest of food.
In regard to	- *With respect to.* He said nothing in regard to your financial position.
In respect of	- *With regard to; detail; particular aspect.* Your essay is admirable in respect of style but unsatisfactory in other respects.

Idioms/Phrases	Usage
In round numbers -	*Approximately*. In round numbers, five thousand people are present in the meeting.
In season and out of season -	*At all times*. He does not appreciate your coming here in season and out of season.
In the event of -	*In case of*. In the event of his transfer, he is prepared to join the new place of posting.
In the face of -	*In the presence of*. What could he do in the face of all these difficulties? He succeeded in the face of great danger (in spite of). He defeated them in the face of all opposition.
In the least -	*In the smallest degree*. It does not matter in the least. I do not understand in the least what this author is trying to say.
In the long run -	*Ultimately*. It pays in the long run to buy goods of high quality.
In the nick of time -	*Only just in time*. They reached the station in the nick of time.
In time -	*Not late; early enough*. We were in time for the train.
In toto -	*Entirely*. He refused to accede to your point of view in toto.
In the prime of life -	*The best part*. He achieved considerable success as a writer in the prime of his life.
In the twinkling of an eye -	*In an instant*. The accident occurred in the twinkling of an eye.
In vogue -	*In fashion, now popular*. This custom is now not in vogue in our country.
Into hot water -	*Get into trouble*. He is responsible for his getting into hot water.
Last but not least -	*Not least in importance*. He is a scholar, an eminent educationist, and last but not least, an honest man.
Length and breadth-	*The whole extent*. Famine spread throughout the length and breadth of the country.

Idioms/Phrases	Usage
Loaves and fishes -	*Personal benefits.* The people in power do not bother about the conditions of the poor; they are concerned mainly with loaves and fishes.
Man of Betters -	*Scholar.* They are all men of Betters.
Man of parts -	*Possessing abilities.* He is a man of parts.
Man of straw -	*A man without substance.* Nobody gives importance to a man of straw.
Now and again -	*Occasionally.* They go to the opera now and again.
Now or never -	*At once; immediately.* Do it now or never.
Null and void -	*Without legal effect, invalid.* The case filed against him was declared null and void by the magistrate.
Of late -	*Lately, recently.* The secret was of late disclosed. Of late he came to realise his folly.
Of no avail -	*Useless.* He was trying to win favour, but it was of no avail. All his plans were of no avail.
Off and on -	*Irregularly, now and again.* It rained off and on all day.
Offhand -	*Without preparation or previous thought.* He used to always give offhand remarks.
Off the point -	*Irrelevantly.* The speaker constantly wanders off the point.
On account -	*Part payment.* The manager of the factory paid the clerk one hundred rupees on account.
On account of -	*Because of.* The college remains closed on account of the summer vacation.
On all fours -	*Exactly similar.* All their problem are on all fours.
On all hands -	*Everywhere.* People admit on all hands that murder is an unpardonable crime.
On an average -	On an average, there are twenty boys present everyday.
On and on -	*Without stopping.* We walked on and on.

Idioms/Phrases	Usage
On one's last legs	*Near one's death or end.* His business is now on its last legs. His condition is so poor that he is now on his last legs.
On the brink of	*Very near to.* He is on the brink of the grave.
On the eve of	*Day or evening before a church festival or any date or event; time just before anything.* My friend invited me to a dinner on the eve of his departure from Cuttack.
On the alert	*Watchful.* You must be on the alert.
On the face of it	*Obviously.* His allegation against you was baseless on the face of it.
Ins and outs	*Full particulars of anything.* They know his ins and outs.
On the look-out	*State of being watchful.* He is on the look-out for bargains.
On the point of	*About to.* He was on the point of leaving for Calcutta.
On the score of	*On account of, in consideration of.* He could not attend the marriage ceremony of his friend on the score of his ill-health.
On the spur of the moment	*On a sudden impulse.* He gave his reply on the spur of the moment.
On the strength of	*Encouraged by, relying upon.* The manager of the factory employed the boy on the strength of your recommendation.
On the wane	*Becoming less or weaker.* His reputation is on the wane.
On the whole	*Taking everything into consideration.* On the whole, he is a fine gentleman.
Once and again	*Now and again, occasionally.* He read the book once and again.
Once for all	*Now and for the last or only time.* He warned them once for all to refrain from cutting jokes with him.
Out of sorts	*Feeling unwell; out of spirits.* He is out of sorts.
Over again	*Once again.* He did the work so badly that I had to do it all over again myself.

Idioms/Phrases	Usage
Over and over again	- *Repeatedly.* I have warned you over and over again not to do that.
Over and above	- *Besides, in addition to.* The waiters get good tips over and above their wages.
Part and parcel	- *An essential part of.* Writing books is a part and parcel of his life. Looking after the downtrodden is a part and parcel of his life. Looking after the downtrodden was a part and parcel of Mother Teresa's life.
Pros and cons	- *Arguments for and against.* He analysed the pros and cons of the matter.
Red-letter day	- *Memorable or fortunate day.* 15th August, 1947 is considered a red-letter day in the history of India.
Root and branch	- *Thoroughly.* All corrupt practices should be removed root and branch.
Stone's throw	- *Very close to.* His residence is within a stone's throw from his office.
Sum and substance	- *General purport.* We know the sum and substance of his speech.
The three R's	- *Reading, writing and arithmetic.* There are people in our country who do not have knowledge of the three R's.
Through and through	- *In all parts; completely.* He is a reliable man through and through. You are wet through and through.
Through thick and thin	- *Under any kind of conditions, good or bad.* He could overcome the difficulties through thick and thin.
Time and again	- *Repeatedly.* He has warned Manindra time and again not to meddle in politics.
Tit for tat	- *Blow for blow.* He was determined to give him tit for tat.
To the contrary	- *To the opposite effect.* I will come on Monday unless you write me to the contrary. I shall continue to believe it until I get proof to the contrary.

Idioms/Phrases		Usage
To the backbone	-	*In every way, thoroughly.* He is an Indian to the backbone. He is a bad man to the backbone.
Under one's thumb	-	*Under somebody's influence and control.* They all know that Ramanendra is under the thumb of the chairman of the corporation.
Under one's very nose	-	*Directly in front of one, in one's presence, and regardless of one's disapproval.* This matter took place under the commissioner's very nose.
Upto the mark	-	*Standard, as good as the normal.* He does not feel quite upto the mark.
Up-to-date	-	*Modern.* Ramesh likes to read up-to-date books on economics.
Wear and tear	-	*Loss; damage from normal use.* You must be prepared for the wear and tear of these materials.
Well and good	-	*A common consequence in a conditional sentence, signifying that the result is satisfactory.* If you get the job, well and good, and if you do not get it, well and good too.
Well off	-	*Lucky, fortunate.* He does not know when he is well off.
Be well out of	-	*Be out of an affair without loss.* You are well out of it.
Well up in	-	*To a considerable extent.* His name is well up in the list (near the top). He is well up in business matters.
Well up for	-	*Well prepared for.* Gopal is not well up for the medical entrance examination.
What not	-	*Various things difficult to mention severally.* He teaches history, geography, English, mathematics and what not.
What's what	-	*What the facts are.* He knows what's what.
What with	-	*Between various causes.* What with overwork and with under-nourishment he fell ill.

Idioms/Phrases	Usage
With a grain of salt	*Feel some doubt whether it is altogether true.* You must take into account his evidence with a grain of salt.
With a view to	*For the purpose of.* He went to the U.S.A. with a view to continuing higher studies in medicine.
With an eye to	*With a view to, hoping for.* He always works hard with an eye to success.
With one accord	*Unanimous.* They are all with one accord in this matter.
Without rhyme or reason	*Without meaning.* He picked up a quarrel with him without any rhyme or reason. He started speaking ill of his friend without rhyme or reason.
Fair-weather friend	*One who befriends only in favourable circumstances.* Bibhudhendra is your fair-weather friend.
To put the change upon a person	*To deceive him.* You cannot put the change on him so easily.
To make two bites of a cherry	*To divide what is so small as scarcely to be worth dividing.* Let's toss up for the seat; there is no use making two bites of a cherry (the seat is too small to accommodate both comfortably).
To call over	*To recite a list.* They were now prevented from further conversation by the arrival of the jailor's servants, who came to call over the prisoner's names.
To call a person to order	*To declare that the person has broken the rules of debates, or is behaving in an unseemly manner.* When a Member of Parliament loses his temper in the House, he is usually called to order by the speaker.
Neat as a pin	*Very neat and tidy.* Everything was as neat as a pin in the house.
In a state of nature	*Naked.* The man, found in the cave, was in a state of nature and raving mad.

Idioms/Phrases		*Usage*
To come to a pretty pass	-	*To be in a bad state.* Things are coming to a pretty pass when you take him to task for not being in earnest.
To pick to pieces	-	*To criticise harshly; to find fault in a jealous fashion.* The ladies were drinking tea, and picking their neighbours to pieces.
To pick a hole in a man's coat	-	*To find fault with a person, to find a weak place in his character.* Umesh performs his duties too faithfully and it is difficult to pick a hole in his coat.
To have a rod in pickle for anyone	-	*To have punishment in store for anyone.* He has a rod in pickle for Bulu when he returns home.
To walk the chalk line	-	*To be particular in one's conduct.* Make him walk the chalk line.
To turn over a new leaf	-	He is determined to turn over a new leaf.
To turn a deaf ear	-	*To ignore.* He turned a deaf ear to their words.
Tell upon	-	*Influence the result of, injure.* All this hard work is telling on him. If you flatter him, it will tell upon your prestige.
To run adrift	-	*Send, cause to go.* He turned his son adrift in the world (sent him away from home without support or help).
To turn the scale	-	*Decide the result of something which is in doubt.* The arrival of reinforcements turned the scale in our favour.
To turn somebody's head	-	*Unsettle; make vain.* All the praise the young actress received turned her head.
To take exception to	-	*To object to; protest against.* He took exception to what I said. She took exception to the statement.
To take somebody to task	-	*Scold him.* It is wrong of you to take the child to task for such trifling offences.

EXERCISE

Make sentences of your own using the following Idioms and Phrases:

All in all, against a rainy day, all and sundry, after all, as a matter of fact, as ill luck would have it, as it were, apple-pie order, abide by, black and blue, bed of roses, crocodile tears, by fits and starts, far from, flesh and blood, from A to Z, in a fix, in respect of, in pursuance of, now or never, of no avail, off and on, well off, under one's thumb, without rhyme or reason, to make two bites of a cherry, to pick a hole in a man's coat, wear and tear, through thick and thin, root and branch, stone's throw, over and above, out of sorts, on the spur of the moment, on one's last legs, off hand, null and void, length and breadth, man of straw, for all the world.

9
PUNCTUATION STOPS OR POINTS

While talking, we do not continue to speak at the same rate. Without thinking of it, we pause every now and then—sometimes very slightly and sometimes for a bit longer. These pauses in speaking help to make clear what we are saying, and without them, our meaning would not always· be understood. Certain signs are used to indicate these speech-pauses. These signs are called "Punctuation Stops or Points". The word 'Punctuation' is derived from a Latin word meaning 'a point'. In fact, punctuation involves putting in correctly the necessary points or stops. The main punctuation stops are (1) The **Full Stop,** or **Period** known by the sign (.), (2) The **Question Stop** by the sign (?), (3) The **Exclamation Stop** by the sign (!), (4) The **Semicolon** by the sign (;), (5) The **Colon** by the sign (:), (6) The **Comma** by the sign (,). Besides these sign, there are also other signs which are used in writing. They are (i) the **Dash (—),** and the **Hyphen (-)** (ii) **Bracket (),** (iii) **Inverted Commas** or **Quotation Marks - Double (" ")** and **Single (' ').**

Since much of the meaning of a sentence depends on putting in these punctuation stops correctly in the context, the writer must be very careful about their correct use. Sometimes wrong punctuation may alter the meaning of a sentence. The punctuation marks which are analysed here should be borne in mind while framing sentences.

1. **The Full Stop or Period (.)**

This indicates (a) the longest pause to mark the end of an Assertive or an Imperative sentence or (b) to mark abbreviations and initials. The following examples show the use of the **full stop:**

   a)   i)   Dear, patient, gentle, noble Charles was dead.

    ii) When you have finished your work, you may go.

    iii) Please take this letter to the post office.

  b)   Govt. = Government; The Hon'ble Minister = The Honourable Minister; Co. Ltd. = Company Limited; B.C. =, Before Christ, etc.

2. The Question Stop (or Note of Interrogation) (?)

Usually this stop is used in place of the full stop after questions or interrogative sentences. It must be borne in mind that question marks are normally put after direct questions. Grammatically speaking, question marks are not used after indirect questions which are actually not questions at all. The following examples show the use of the **question stops:**

    i)   Has the train reached Delhi?

    ii) Who are you? What are you doing? Where have you been?

    iii) When you have finished your work, are you going straight home?

3. The Exclamation Stop or Note of Exclamation (!)

This mark is normally used in place of the full stop after Interjections, Exclamations, and Exclamatory sentences. One must be very careful about the use of exclamation marks, for it should not be used too much in English. The learner must take adequate care to use them only after real exclamations and sometimes after short and peremptory commands. The following examples indicate the use of these marks:

    i)   Oh! Alas! Bravo! Hurrah! Hear, hear!

        How sad! What a shame! Well done!

        How well he spoke today!

    ii) O that I had wings like a dove!

    iii) Long live the king!

    iv) 'Get out! I don't want to see you again!'

    v) 'Oh dear! What am I going to do?'

4. The Semicolon (;)

It marks a pause not so long as that marked by the full stop, but longer than that marked by the comma. Thus it is a lesser stop than the full stop and is used between grammatically complete sentences. It is not followed by a capital letter and is often found before such connective words as, 'and', 'but', 'or'. It is used (a) to separate a series of loosely related clauses (b) to separate the clauses of a long sentence when they contain commas. The following examples indicate the use of semicolon marks:

a) i) I came; I saw; I conquered.
    ii) A rogue I hate; a fool I despise; a weakling I pity; an honest person I love.
b) i) He was honest, punctual and hardworking; still, in spite of this, I never liked him.
    ii) That he was a brave man, no one ever doubted; that he was also wise, is not so certain.
    iii) He also told me about his grandfather; but that is another story.
    iv) The family is going for a picnic; father carries the rugs; mother the food; and the children, the rest of the things.

5. The Colon (:)

This punctuation stop is not much used now, except to mark off a direct quotation. It is normally used to mark a still longer pause than that marked by the semicolon. The colon is used (a) to introduce a quotation, (b) before a list on enumeration or examples, (c) to introduce an explanation, (d) to introduce an amplification. The following examples indicate the use of the colon:

a) i) The Bible tells us: "God is love".
    ii) The proverb says: "Waste not, want not".
        In the use of such colon marks, sometimes a dash (—) is used after the colon (:); as, Your brother writes: "I am going to Delhi."
b) i) The principal parts of a verb are: the present tense, the past tense and the past participle.
    ii) You must now hear about the uses of iron: we sleep on iron; we travel on iron; we float on iron; we plough the fields with iron; we shoot with iron; we cut down the trees with iron.
    iii) These are the things we shall need: flask of coffee, some sandwiches, and some fruit.
    iv) The reason he gave was this: he had not properly understood the instructions.
    v) You must consult a good dictionary, such as: *The Oxford, Webster's* or *Chambers'*.

6. The Comma (,)

This is the slightest pause in natural speaking. In general, it is used whenever a very slight pause would be necessary in the saying or reading of a sentence, for reasons of sense or sound. It is used to separate the principal clause preceded by a subordinate clause of any sort. It is used to separate short coordinate clauses of a compound sentence.

a) i) It being now late, he went back home.
   ii) He is , in my opinion, the best man for the job.
   iii) We want help, not mere sympathy.

b) i) When you are ready, we shall go.
   ii) If you can't understand, tell me.
   iii) If you want to be happy, don't make enemies.
   iv) That he would succeed in the end, no one ever doubted.
   v) The minstrel was infirm and old.
   vi) Men may come, and men may go.

c) The comma is used before and after
   i) words and phrases in apposition
   ii) it is used to separate off the absolute constructions from the rest of the sentence
   iii) to separate the adjectival phrases made with participles when they are non-defining from the rest of the sentence:
     i) Mr. Jones, the Mayor of Casterbridge, said...
     Milton, the great English poet, was blind.
     ii) Dinner over, they rose to go back to the sitting room.
     iii) The speaker, getting to his feet, began to address the audience.

d) It is used to separate words of the same parts of speech in a sentence; as, soldiers, sailors, miners, and firemen must all have courage.

e) It is used to mark off a Nominative of Address; as, I tell you, my dear man, you are wasting your time.

f) It is used to mark off a participle phrase; as, The wind being favourable, the ship sailed.

g) It is used before and after words, phrases and clauses introduced into the body of the sentence; as, The mango tree, which was in fruit at the time, was blown down.

h) It is used to mark the omission of a word, especially a verb; as, He will succeed; you, never.

i) Commas can also be used in lists of all sorts except where the words are arranged in pairs or joined by 'and' or 'or', as,
   i) I shall need a hammer, a saw, some nails, and a piece of wood.

ii) We wash our hands with soap and water.

iii) By car or bus, by rail or air, they all came to the capital to see the exhibition.

j) Such words as 'too', 'however', 'nevertheless', 'though, 'of course', 'then' are normally enclosed in commas if they are used in the middle or at the end of a sentence; as,

He, however, has never made that mistake.

You, too, can have a Maruti car like Nikhilesh's.

k) If we want to place adverbs or adverbial expressions in an unusual position in the sentence, we have to enclose them in commas; as,

Your friend has, since his wedding, not been seen at the club.

Those people tried, in spite of my advice, to climb the mountain.

l) Commas may be used to mark off quotations from the rest of the sentence; as,

He said to his disciples, "Watch and pray."

7. Inverted Commas (" ") and (' ').

These are used to enclose a quotation, or the exact words of the speaker; as,

The *Bible* says: "Blessed are the merciful".

If a quotation is used within a quotation, it is marked by single inverted commas; as,

"You might as well say," added the March Hare, that 'I like what I get' is the same thing as "I get what I like."

8. The Dash (—) and the Hyphen (-)

The dash is used (a) to mark off a sudden stop or change of thought or (b) to sum up several subjects, all belonging to the same verb.

a) If his father were—but why talk of the past?

b) Friends, companions, relatives—all deserted him.

The hyphen (-), a shorter line than the dash (—), is used to connect the parts of a compound word; as,

Jack-of-all-trades; man-of-parts; happy-go-lucky, etc. The hyphen is also used to connect parts of a word divided at the end of a line; as, Pre-vented; en-gineer; call-ing.

9. Brackets (or Double Dashes)

These are used to separate from the main part of the sentence a phrase or clause which does not grammatically belong to it; as,

   i)   He gained from Heaven (it was all he asked) a friend.

   ii) A striking example of this kind of courage—call it, if you
       please, strong will—is given in the history of Rana Pratap.

10. **Use of Capital Letters**

     The capital letters must be used

   a)   At the beginning of every new sentence: as,
       She came home. The horse is lame.
       Where is your uncle?

   b)   To begin a proper noun; as,
       Christian, Muslim, Clive, India, Sunday, August, etc.

   c)   For interjections, and the beginning of quotations; as,
       i) Oh! Alas! My God!
       ii) The proverb says, "All that glitters, is not gold".

   d)   For degrees, titles, etc.; as,
       Master of Arts, His Excellency, Your Highness, Your
       Majesty, etc.

   e)   At the beginning of every line of verse; as,
       A damsel with a dulcimer,
       In a vision once I saw,
       It was an Abyssinian maid,
       And on her dulcimer she played.

EXERCISES

1.   Place commas, where necessary, in the following sentences:

   a) He is moreover an all-round scholar.

   b) The traffic police said "Keep to the left".

   c) If you go to Cuttack you will see him.

   d) Nirmal Babu gave the poor man food clothes money and
      work.

   e) Ramesh his eldest son left this college.

   f) He likes French literature which he is always talking about.

   g) When they come tell them to wait for sometime.

   h) Until you accede to his point of view he will not leave you.

   i) Gentleman I thank you heartily.

   j) Where do you stay Amlan?

2.   Punctuate the following sentences:

   i) You and I are mortal so are all men of the world

   ii) They met sisir nitais brother both in madras and hyderabad
      he was he said on a study tour

iii) The shepherd finding his flock destroyed exclaimed i have been rightly punished why did i trust my sheep to a wolf

iv) He came to understand in course of time that the man to whom he confided his secret was unreliable and harmful

v) there was once a poor man who could no longer maintain his only son then said the son dear father things are so bad that i feel i am a burden to you i would rather go forth and seek some way of earning my bread his father thereupon gave him his blessing and with great sorrow took leave of him

vi) You have to cross chilika to visit parikud

vii) When you have finished your work are you going straight home

viii) He was honest punctual hard-working still in spite of this i never liked him

ix) these are the things we shall need a flask of coffee some sandwiches and some fruit

x) by car or bus by rail or air they all came to the capital to see the exhibition

xi) he said to his disciples watch and pray

xii) a striking example of this kind of courage call it if you please strong will is given in the history of rana pratap.

10
PHRASES AND CLAUSES IDENTICAL IN MEANING

What are Phrases and Clauses and what is the difference between them? Look at the following sentences:
1. At sunset the farmers returned home.
2. When the sun set the farmers returned home.

In sentence (1), the group of words 'at sunset' makes some sense but does not contain a predicate either expressed or understood. Hence it is a Phrase. In sentence (2), the group of words, 'when the sun set' is not a Phrase, because it has a subject, 'the sun' and a predicate 'set when', of its own and it forms part of a larger sentence. Hence it is a clause. Further, the second sentence, 'when the sun set the farmers returned home' contains two parts or clauses and each part or clause in the sentence has a subject and a predicate of its own. Since a phrase is distinguished from a clause, we can define them in the following manner:-

A Phrase may be defined as a group of words that makes sense but not complete sense because it has neither a subject nor a predicate.

A Clause may be defined as a group of words forming part of a larger sentence, and having a Subject and a Predicate of its own.

A. Phrases

There are seven kinds of phrases. They are: (1) Noun Phrase, (2) Adjective Phrase, (3) Adverb Phrase, (4) Absolute Phrase, (5) Prepositional Phrase, (6) Conjunctional Phrase, and (7) Interjectional Phrase.

1. Noun Phrase
Look at the following sentences:
i) He told them *to see him in the morning.*

ii) *To obey your parents* is your first duty.

iii) He likes *swimming in the hot weather*.

Here in sentences (i), (ii) and (iii), the phrases 'to see him in the morning', 'to obey your parents' and 'swimming in the hot water' are used as objects to the verbs 'told', 'is' and 'likes' respectively. These phrases are called Noun Phrases because they do the work of nouns.

2. **Adjective Phrase**
Look at the words in italics in the following sentences:

i) Narendra is in *very good health.*

ii) Dinesh holds a post *of great importance.*

iii) He has a dog *with a long tail.*

In sentences (i), (ii) and (iii), the phrases 'in very good health', 'of great importance', and 'with a long tail' add something to the meaning of the noun with which they are used and which they qualify. These phrases do the work of adjectives and therefore, they are called Adjective Phrases.

3. **Adverb Phrase**
Look at the phrases in the following sentences:

i) He spoke *in a very loud voice.*

ii) They will come *in a little while.*

iii) I read the letter *on my way to the office.*

In the above sentences (i), (ii) and (iii), the phrases 'in a very loud voice', 'in a little while', and 'on my way to the office' answer the questions 'how', 'when' and 'where' respectively. They do the work of adverbs and therefore, they can be called Adverb Phrases.

4. **Absolute or Unrelated Phrase**
Look at the following sentences:

i) *God willing,* our country will prosper.

ii) *The meeting over,* they all went away.

iii) *His mother being ill,* he cannot come to the college.

iv) *The rain having stopped,* the workers came back to their respective houses.

The words in italics in each of the above sentences are phrases. They stand alone and are independent of themselves. They are also unrelated to the other parts of the sentence. They can, therefore, be called Absolute Phrases.

5. **Prepositional Phrase**
A Prepositional Phrase does the work of a preposition; as,

He succeeded *by virtue* of his talents.
You are senior to him *in point of age.*

6. **Conjunctional Phrases**
A Conjunctional Phrase does the work of a conjunction; as,
He took medicine *in order that* he might recover.
The students were silent *as soon as* the teacher entered the room.

7. **Interjectional Phrase**
An Interjectional Phrase does the work of an interjection; as,
What a pity!
For shame!
Now, look at the following sentences:
He is fond of *playing tennis.*
(Noun Phrase, object to 'of')
The boys *playing tennis* are his sons. (Adjective Phrase qualifying 'boys')
He stood on *the burning deck.* (Adverbial Phrase modifying 'stood')
The man *on the burning deck* was quite alone.
(Adjective Phrase qualifying 'man')
These sentences indicate that the same phrase may be used as a Noun Phrase in one sentence and an Adjective or an Adverbial Phrase in another, according to whether it does the work of a Noun or an Adjective or an Adverb.
Look at these sentences as given below:
A friend in need is a friend indeed.
(Noun Phrase, subject to the verb 'is')
A friend *in need* is a friend indeed.
(Adjective Phrase qualifying 'friend')
The train was delayed *on account of* the accident.
(Adverbial Phrase)
The train was delayed *on its own count.*
(Prepositional Phrase)
The above sentences show that the group of words forming the whole phrase may sometimes differ in use from the group of words forming the part.

B) **Clauses.**
Look at the following sentences:

1. The assassin died *before his trial.*
2. The assassin died *before he was tried.*
3. He saw a tiger *while going on the road.*
4. He saw a tiger when he was going on the road.
5. *The meeting being over,* they all went away.
6. They all went away when the meeting was over.

In sentences 1, 3, and 5, 'before his trial', 'while going on the road' and 'the meeting being over' are groups of words attached to these sentences respectively. They are not sentences and as such they do not make complete sense. Only the groups of words in italics have a meaning and make some sense. But they have neither a subject nor a predicate of their own. They can be called phrases. But in sentences 2, 4, and 6, each sentence is a larger sentence and has two sentences or parts of its own. Thus, the sentence contains two parts, the assassin died' and 'before his trial'. Each of these parts has a subject and a predicate of its own and each part is independent of itself and makes complete sense. Such a group of words which has a subject and a predicate of its own and forms a part of a larger sentence is called a clause. Thus in sentence 2, 'the assassin died' and 'he was tried' are two clauses joined by the word 'before'. Similarly in sentence 4, 'He saw a tiger' and 'he was going on the road' are two clauses or parts of a larger sentence, 'He saw a tiger, when he was going on the road' and these two clauses or parts are joined by the word 'when'. In sentence 6, there are two clauses such as, 'They all went away' and 'the meeting was over' and these two parts are joined by the word 'when'. Thus these two parts or clauses are parts of a larger sentence. We may define a clause as a group of words having a subject and a predicate of its own and forming a part of a larger sentence.

There are three kinds of sentences such as (1) simple, (2) complex, and (3) compound.

1) A sentence having one finite verb is called a simple sentence. The following sentences illustrate this point:
   i) He returned.
   ii) He enjoyed his holidays.
   iii) You are looking very fine today.

In sentences (i), (ii) and (iii), each has only one finite verb and sentences (ii) and (iii) are longer than the sentence (i). Thus it is evident from these sentences that a simple sentence may have only two words or even one such as 'Stop'. However long a simple sentence may be, it must have only one finite verb.

2) A complex sentence has one principal or main clause and one or more subordinate or dependent clauses.

Look at the following sentences:

i) This is the mongoose *which killed the snake*.

ii) *When the meeting was over*, they all went home.

iii) The students could not hear *what the teacher said*.

Each of these sentences has two finite verbs. In sentence (i) 'is' and 'killed', in sentence (ii) 'was' and 'went' and in sentence (iii) 'could hear' and 'said'. Further, each sentence has two clauses and the clause in italics depends on the other. In sentence (i), the clause 'which killed the snake' does not make complete sense itself without the other clause, 'this is the mongoose'. The same is true of 'when the meeting was over' in sentence (ii) and 'what the teacher said' in sentence (iii). Thus it is evident that each of these clauses is subordinate to the other clause in the sentence. Such clauses (which depend on another) are called *subordinate* or *dependent clauses*. The principal or independent clause does not depend on a clause or clauses and can stand by itself. It makes complete sense independently.

There are three kinds of subordinate clauses such as (1) Noun Clause, (2) Adjective Clause, and (3) Adverb Clause.

1. Noun Clause

A Noun Clause does the work of a noun. The following examples indicate the use of Noun Clauses:

i) I expect *that he will get the prize*.

ii) *That you have come* pleases me.

iii) *What you told him* was not true.

In the first sentence, the clause 'that he will get the prize' is the object of the verb 'expect' and so does the work of a noun. The clauses in the second and third sentences are subjects of the verbs 'pleases' and 'was' respectively, and as such do the work of nouns. They are, therefore, called Noun Clauses.

2. Adjective Clause

An Adjective Clause does the work of an adjective. The following examples indicate the use of Adjective Clauses:

i) Here is the man *whom you wanted to see*.

ii)   God helps those *who help themselves.*

iii) He spends all *that he earns.*

In the above sentences, the clauses given in italics qualify the noun in the first sentence and the pronoun in the last two sentences. They are, therefore, called Adjective Clauses.

3.   Adverb Clause

An Adverb Clause does the work of an adverb. The following examples show the use of Adverb Clauses:

i)   We rested *when the sun had set.*

ii) He was eating *when Subhendu called.*

iii) They went *where they could find work.*

In the above sentences, the clauses given in italics modify the verbs 'rested', 'was eating' and 'went', indicating at the same time 'when' in the first two sentences and 'where' in the last sentence the actions were done. Thus it is clear that Adverb Clauses, like adverbs, answer the questions, when? where? how? Why? etc. They are, therefore, called Adverb Clauses.

In complex sentences, the Noun Clause does the work of a noun. It can be used as,

i)   The subject of a verb; as,
      When he will return is uncertain.

ii) The object of a Transitive verb; as,
      Rakesh denied *that he had stolen the book.*

iii) The object of a preposition; as,
      Pay attention to *what he is saying.*

iv) The complement of a verb of Incomplete Predication; as,
      The trouble is *that he has lost the wrist watch.*

v)   In apposition to a noun or pronoun; as,
      His statement *that he lost the money* will not be believed.
      It is unfortunate *that Bimal was absent.*

An Adjective Clause is normally introduced by a relative pronoun or a relative adverb; as,

He is a man *whom* they all respect.

The wall clock *that* you gave me has been stolen.

The time *when* the aeroplane leaves is not yet known.

The reason *why* he did it is very clear.

But sometimes the relative pronoun or the relative adverb introducing an Adjective Clause is understood; as,

Eat all *you can.* (that)

Is this the man *you want to see?* (whom)

On the day *you pass the examination,* your father will give you a present. (when)

The reason *he went back* was to ask for his money. (why)

Adverb Clauses are of many kinds. The following examples indicate the use of Adverb Clauses in various ways:

When you are ready, they will start (time).

They went where they could find work (place).

It all ended *as we expected (manner).*

They ran away *because they were afraid* (cause).

He studies hard *so that he may pass* (purpose).

It is clear from the above examples that different kinds of Adverb Clauses are introduced by the subordinating conjunctions of time, place, manner, cause and purpose, etc.

The following sentences indicate that sometimes phrases can be replaced by clauses and *vice versa* without any change in meaning:

a) Noun Phrases replaced by Noun Clauses.

Ramesh expected *to win the first prize.* (Noun Phrase)

Ramesh expected *that he would win the first prize.* (Noun Clause)

They cannot guess *the reason for his failure.* (Noun Phrase)

They cannot guess *why he has failed.* (Noun Clause)

He hoped *for better times.* (Noun Phrase)

He hoped *that better times would come.* (Noun Clause)

The following sentences show that Noun Clauses can be replaced by Noun Phrases:

i) The rumour *that the Chairman of the Planning Commission has resigned* is false. (Noun Clause)

The rumour *about the resignation of the Chairman of the Planning Commission* is false. (Noun Phrase)

ii) It is not known *when he was born.* (Noun Clause)

The time of his birth is not known. (Noun Phrase)

iii) We don't doubt *that he is honest.* (Noun Clause)

We don't doubt *his honesty.* (Noun Phrase)

b) Adjective Phrases replaced by Adjective Clauses.

i) He likes flowers *with a sweet fragrance.* (Adjective Phrase)

He likes flowers *which have a sweet fragrance.* (Adjective Clause)

ii) He has a dog *with a long tail.* (Adjective Phrase)

He has a dog *which has a long tail.* (Adjective Clause)

iii) He has a house *to let.* (Adjective Phrase)

He has a house *that can be let.* (Adjective Clause)

iv) A man *having the fewest wants* is the happiest. (Adjective Phrase)

He is the happiest man *who has the fewest wants.* (Adjective Clause)

The following sentences indicate that Adjective Clauses can be replaced by Adjective Phrases:

i) He is not a man *who can accept bribes.* (Adjective Clause)

He is not a man *to accept bribes.* (Adjective Phrase)

ii) He was absent at the time *when this occurred.* (Adjective Clause)

He was absent *at the time of this occurrence.* (Adjective Phrase)

c) Adverbial Phrases replaced by Adverbial Clauses:

i) *In his absence,* they opened his house. (Adverbial Phrase)

They opened his house *when he was absent.* (Adverbial Clause)

ii) He did the work *to the best of his ability.* (Adverbial Phrase)

He did the work *as well as he could.* (Adverbial Clause)

iii) They changed their clothes *for fear of detection.* (Adverbial Phrase)

They changed their clothes *lest they should be detected.* (Adverbial Clause)

The following sentences indicate that Adverbial Clauses can be replaced by Adverbial Phrases:

i) They have performed their duties *better than he expected.* (Adverbial Clause)

They have performed their duties *beyond his expectation.* (Adverbial Phrase)

ii) He worked hard *that he might get a scholarship.* (Adverbial Clause)

He worked hard *for the purpose of getting a scholarship.* (Adverbial Phrase)

iii) *As the committee has already arrived at a decision,* further evidence was useless. (Adverbial Clause)

The committee having already arrived at a decision, further evidence was useless. (Adverbial Phrase)

EXERCISES

1. Substitute Phrases for the Clauses given in italics in the following sentences:
   a) They waited at the bus stand *until the rain ceased.*
   b) *As you sow,* so you will reap.
   c) He is hopeful *that his brother will soon recover.*
   d) He completed his high school education in *the village where he was born.*
   e) He was appointed Chairman of the Corporation *because the Chief Minister recommended him.*
   f) God helps those *who help the poor.*
   g) *As soon as he reached there,* he saw his friend.
   h) It is said *that the headman of the village died of jaundice.*
   i) He wanted to know *where his friend, Nitish, lived in Calcutta.*
   j) He was unwilling to admit the fact *that he told lies to them.*

2. Substitute Clauses for the Phrases in italics in the following sentences:
   i) They found no place *to rest at night.*
   ii) *Your offence* is unpardonable.
   iii) *Notwithstanding his sincere efforts* he could not do well in the examination.
   iv) *But for your help* he would have suffered much.
   v) They took a decision *to lend their support to us.*
   vi) The temple *in front of his house* was constructed by his grandfather.
   vii) The man fought the tiger *with all his might.*
   viii) *At sunset,* they all returned home.
   ix) They cannot guess the *reason for his failure.*
   x) *In his absence* they opened his house.

11
SPELLING

Spelling forms an important part of written language. When we speak or in our spoken language, the spelling of a word/ words does not make a difference to the person/persons to whom we address our speech or with whom we hold our discourse. There is no scope of letting the hearers know the spelling of the words we use in the sentences of our conversation or speech nor does the hearer have the scope of knowing whether it is correct or not. But in our writing we become very careful about spelling of words. Sometimes it is found that the learner, because of his carelessness in spelling of words, tends to commit errors. Therefore, adequate attention must be given to spelling while using words in sentences. There are some important rules about spelling which must be borne in mind. The following are some important rules with examples:

Rule 1. If the final consonant in a word or words of one syllable is preceded by a single vowel, it is usually doubled before the suffixes -ing, -ed, etc.; as, sit— sitting, sitter; rot—rotting, rotted; jog—jogging, jogged; hum—humming, hummed; nod—nodding, nodded; pat—patting, patted; fit—fitting, fitted; rob—robbing, robbed, robber; map—mapping, mapped; mat—matting, matted; rag—ragging, ragged; knit—knitting, knitter, knitted; label— labelling, labelled; nag—nagging, nagger, nagged; drop—dropping, dropped; ship—shipping, lug— luggage; big—bigger; win—winner, winning; mud— muddy; run—running, runners; sun—sunny, etc.

Rule 2. If the final consonant in a word or words of two or, more than two syllables is preceded by a single vowel, it is normally doubled before the suffixes -ing, -ed, etc., and in such a case the accent is on the last syllable; as, begin—beginning, beginner; permit—permitting, permitted; occur—occurring, occurred; remit—remitting, remitter, remitted; submit—submitting, submitted; befit—befitting, befitted; refer—referring, referred; commit—committing, committed; regret—regretted, regrettable; omit—omitted; confer—conferring, conferred, etc.

Rule 3. If the final consonant is preceded by more than one vowel, it is not doubled; as, root—rooted; weep—weeping; cool—cooling, cooled; gain—gaining, gained; keep—keeping; read—reading; soar—soaring, soared; wood—wooden; sweet—sweeten; boil—boiling, boiled; feed—feeding; beat—beating, beaten; read—reading; reap—reaping, reaped; lean—leaning, leaned; wait—waiting, waited; seat—seating, seated.

Exceptions: Wool—woollen; quit—quitting; swim—swimming; acquit—acquitted.

Rule 4. If the last syllable is not accented, the final consonant is not doubled; as, alter—altering, altered; benefit—benefiting, benefited; offer—offering, offered; profit—profiting, profited; suffer—suffering, suffered; visit—visiting, visited.

Exceptions: Parallel—parallelled or paralleled; worship—worshipping, worshipped.

Rule 5. When such words as 'all' and 'full' are added to some other words, normally one 'l' is dropped; as, almighty, already, always, fulfil, fulsome, mouthful, truthful, useful, altogether, youthful, powerful, colourful.

Exceptions: All-powerful, full-grown, fullness or fulness.

Rule 6. If the words ending in 'll' are added to some other words, they retain both these two letters; as, bell-shaped, dull-brained, farewell, hilltop, nut-shell, roll-call, spellbound, stillness, telltale, unwell, waterfall, well-being, well-known, hell-bound.

Exceptions: Dulness or dullness, skilful, until, welcome, welfare, wilful.

Rule 7.   The letter 'c' is almost always followed by 'ei', but other letters are normally followed by 'ie'; as, ceiling, conceive, conceit, deceive, deceit, receive, receipt; achieve, believe, belief, brief, grief, niece, siege, yield, shield.

Exceptions: Deity, forfeit, height, leisure, seize, reign, weight, etc.

Rule 8.   The final 'e' in some words is sometimes dropped before certain suffixes; as, argue—argument; awe— awful; drive—driving; due—duly; move—movable; love—lovable; pursue—pursuing; true—truly; value—valuable; write—writing.

Rule 9.   Words ending in 'ee' or 'ye' do not drop the final 'e' before suffixes; as, agree—agreeing, agreeable; flee— fleeing; see—seeing; dye—dyeing.

Rule 10.   Words ending in 'ce' or 'ge' seldom drop the final 'e'; as, practice—practicable; malice—malicious; *but* apprentice—apprenticeship; service—serviceable; acknowledge—acknowledgement;   judge— judgment. *But* change—changeable, charge— chargeable; courage—courageous; manage— manageable, management; marriage—marriageable.

Rule 11.   Normally the final 'y' preceded by a consonant or consonants is changed into 'i' before certain suffixes; as, beauty—beautiful; cry—cries, cried; happy—happiness; lucky—luckily; merry—merrily, merriment; mighty—mightier; pity—pitiable; rely— reliance, reliable; supply—supplied; apply—applied; beautify—beautified; nullify—nullified; worthy— worthiest; lovely—loveliest; carry—carried; hurry— hurried; fury—furious.

Exceptions: Copy—copyist; fly—flying; lady—ladyship; try— trying; sky—skyish.

Rule 12.   If the final letter 'y' in a word is preceded by a vowel. it is not normally changed into 'i'; as, buy—buying, buyer; convey—conveyance; joy—joyous; pay— paying, payee; play—playing, player; pray—prays, prayed, prayer; key—keys; way—ways; valley— valleys; day—days; donkey—donkeys; monkey— monkeys; say—saying.

Exceptions: Pay—paid; say—said.

Rule 13. Words of one syllable having only one vowel letter do not end with the single consonant -s, -f, -c, -l -z. Miss, cliff, pull, jazz, brass, pass, puff, stiff, lull, whizz, kiss, fizz, hell, pill, gill, bell, fell, well, staff, still, fill, full, stuff, buzz, etc.

Exceptions: This, his, if, bus, us, has.

Rule 14. Words having one syllable and one vowel letters cannot end in 'c' alone but use '-ck'; as, luck, back, sick, thick, hack, jack, buck, kick, sack, lack, mock, tack, tick, tuck, cock, crack, deck, dock, duck, lock, lick, mack, muck, knack, nick, knock, pack, pick, puck, rack, rock, rick, ruck, wick, wreck, trick. But words of one syllable with two vowel letters cannot end in '-ck', but require '-k' alone; as, leak, steak, beak, look, book, weak, rook, seek.

EXERCISES

1. Write the Past and Past Participles of the following words:

shrug	hum	whip	rot
submit	hid	knit	rod
commit	slam	mat	pat
befit	drop	map	rag
sag	ship	fit	rob
permit	occur	forget	label
compel	regret	admit	confer
remit	refer	omit	nag
repel			

2. Write the Plural forms of the following words:

glory	victory	cry	monkey
jelly	body	donkey	study
reply	way	sympathy	key
storey	baby	valley	day
joy	berry	fury	supply
chimney	dormitory	turkey	laboratory

3. Write the Present and Past Participles of the following Verbs:

delay	hurry	rely	dry
supply	try	play	display

apply	marry	convey	deny
reply	nullify	study	qualify
carry	multiply	sway	purify
destroy	beautify	annoy	modify
pray	enjoy	fry	

12
ANTONYMS AND SYNONYMS

A) Antonyms

An antonym signifies the word of contrary meaning to another as 'bad' to 'good'. It is the opposite of a synonym which refers to a word or phrase identical and coextensive in sense and usage with another of the same language or denotes the same thing or things as another but suitable to a different context. Thus an antonym is opposite in meaning to another. Some words and their antonyms are as follows:

Words	Antonyms	Words	Antonyms
Ability	Inability	Allow	Disallow
Able	Unable	Always	Never
Above	Below	Ambiguous	Clear
Absent	Present	Analysis	Synthesis
Abundance	Dearth	Ancient	Modern
Accept	Reject	Angel	Devil
Accord	Discord	Animate	Inanimate
Acquit	Convict	Appear	Disappear
Act	Counteract	Appreciate	Depreciate
Action	Inaction	Arrival	Departure
Active	Inactive	Arrogant	Humble
Admit	Deny	Ascend	Descend
Adopt	Reject	Ascent	Descent
Adroit	Maladroit	Assemble	Disperse
Adult	Child	Assent	Dissent
Advantage	Disadvantage	Asset	Liability
Adversity	Prosperity	Associate	Dissociate
Affirm	Deny	Attach	Detach
Affluence	Poverty	Attack	Protect
Agree	Disagree	Attentive	Inattentive

Words	Antonyms	Words	Antonyms
Attract	Repel	Complete	Incomplete
Bad	Good	Compress	Expand
Barbarous	Civilised	Conceal	Reveal
Barren	Fertile	Condemn	Approve,
Base	Apex, Noble		acquit
Beautiful	Ugly	Confident	Diffident
Beginning	End	Contraction	Expansion
Belief	Disbelief	Cool	Warm
Believe	Disbelieve	Correct	Incorrect
Benediction	Malediction	Courageous	Cowardly
Benefactor	Malefactor	Create	Destroy
Benefit	Harm	Cruel	Kind, merciful
Benevolence	Malevolence	Danger	Safety
Better	Worse	Dark	Light
Big	Small	Dawn	Dusk
Birth	Death	Day	Night
Blame	Praise	Dead	Alive
Bold	Timid	Death	Life
Bottom	Top	Debit	Credit
Bravery	Cowardice	Debt	Credit
Bright	Dark, dull	Decent	Indecent
Broad	Narrow	Decrease	Increase
Brutal	Human	Deep	Shallow
Buy	Sell	Defendant	Plaintiff
Calm	Excited	Defensive	Offensive
Capture	Release	Deficit	Surplus
Care	Neglect	Definite	Vague
Cause	Effect	Deflate	Inflate
Cheap	Dear,	Delay	Haste
	expensive	Delete	Insert
Cheerful	Gloomy,	Delight	Sorrow
	cheerless	Departure	Arrival
Civilisation	Barbarism	Dependent	Independent
Clean	Dirty	Deposit	Withdraw
Clever	Stupid	Descend	Ascend
Cold	Hot	Despair	Hope
Comic	Tragic	Destructive	Constructive
Common	Uncommon,	Difficult	Easy
	rare	Diligent	Idle
Compatible	Incompatible	Diminish	Increase

Words	Antonyms	Words	Antonyms
Discourage	Encourage	Fertile	Barren, sterile
Disease	Health	Float	Sink
Domestic	Wild	Folly	Wisdom
Doubtful	Sure, certain	Foolish	Wise
Dry	Wet	Foreign	Native
Dwarf	Tall	Fortune	Misfortune
Early	Late	Freedom	Slavery
Earthly	Heavenly, celestial	Fresh	Stale
		Friend	Foe
Effect	Cause	Friendly	Hostile
Empty	Full	Falsehood	Truth
Encourage	Discourage	Flexible	Rigid
Enmity	Friendship	Forgiveness	Punishment
Enrich	Impoverish	Formal	Informal
Enthusiasm	Indifference	Former	Latter
Entrance	Exit	Frank	Reticent
Equal	Unequal	Friendship	Enmity
Equality	Inequality	Front	Back
Esteem	Contempt	Frugality	Prodigality
Evil	Good	Gain	Loss
Exclude	Include	General	Particular
Expire	Live	Generous	Niggardly
Explicit	Implicit	Gentle	Ungentle, rough
Exterior	Interior		
Extraordinary	Ordinary	Genuine	False
Extravagant	Frugal, economical, thrifty	Give	Take
		Gloomy	Gay
		Godly	Godless
Fact	Fiction	Gorgeous	Modest
Failure	Success	Great	Small
Fair	Foul	Guilty	Innocent
Faithful	Faithless	Half	Full
Fall	Rise	Happiness	Unhappiness, sorrow
False	True		
Familiar	Unfamiliar, strange	Hard	Soft
		Harsh	Gentle
Famous	Notorious	Hate	Love
Far	Near	Healthy	Sick
Fast	Slow	Heaven	Hell
Fat	Thin, lean	Heavy	Light

Words	Antonyms	Words	Antonyms
Help	Hinder	Last	First
Hero	Villain	Later	Earlier
High	Low	Latitude	Longitude
Hollow	Solid	Latter	Former
Honest	Dishonest	Lawful	Unlawful
Honour	Shame	Lazy	Industrious
Hope	Despair	Lead	Lag, follow
Host	Guest	Legal	Illegal
Huge	Small	Legible	Illegible
Humble	Proud,	Legitimate	Illegitimate
	haughty	Lend	Borrow
Hurt	Heal	Liberal	Illiberal
Ignorance	Knowledge	Light	Heavy
Import	Export	Like	Dislike
Important	Unimportant,	Literate	Illiterate
	trivial	Living	Dead
Improvement	Deterioration	Logical	Illogical
Inanimate	Animate	Long	Short
Incapable	Capable	Loose	Tight
Include	Exclude	Loud	Low
Income	Expenditure	Loyal	Disloyal
Incomplete	Complete	Major	Minor
Increase	Decrease	Mandatory	Optional
Indecent	Decent	Masculine	Feminine
Individual	Species	Master	Servant
Inferior	Superior	Material	Immaterial,
Infinite	Finite		spiritual
Infringe	Obey	Mature	Immature
Ingress	Egress	Maximum	Minimum
Inhale	Exhale	Meagre	Plentiful
Injustice	Justice	Merit	Demerit
Innocent	Guilty	Mighty	Feeble
Insert	Extract	Miser	Spendthrift
Interested	Disinterested	Miserly	Generous
Introduce	Conclude	Mobile	Immobile,
Join	Disjoin		stationary
Joy	Sorrow	Moderate	Immoderate
Junior	Senior	Moral	Immoral
Justice	Injustice	Motion	Rest, inertia
Languid	Energetic	Movable	Immovable

Words	Antonyms	Words	Antonyms
Natural	Unnatural, artificial	Profound	Frivolous
		Promptly	Slowly
Neat	Untidy	Proper	Improper
Negative	Positive	Proud	Humble
New	Old	Public	Private
Noble	Ignoble	Punctual	Late, unpunctual
Normal	Abnormal		
Obedient	Disobedient	Punishment	Reward
Obtain	Forfeit	Pure	Impure
Often	Seldom	Push	Pull
Old	New	Quarrelsome	Friendly
Ominous	Auspicious	Queer	Ordinary
Optimist	Pessimist	Question	Answer
Oral	Written	Quick	Slow, tardy
Order	Disorder	Quiet	Noisy
Pardon	Chastise	Rare	Common
Partial	Impartial	Rebuke	Praise
Passionate	Dispassionate	Recover	Lose, forfeit
Past	Present	Refund	Withhold
Peace	War	Regular	Irregular
Perfect	Imperfect	Reject	Accept
Permanent	Temporary	Religious	Irreligious
Persuade	Dissuade	Remember	Forget
Pleasant	Unpleasant	Remote	Near
Please	Displease	Rapidity	Inertia
Pleasure	Pain, displeasure	Rash	Steady
		Receive	Give
Plenty	Paucity, scarcity	Refute	Confirm
		Repulsive	Attractive
Polite	Impolite, rude	Resistible	Irresistible
		Rich	Poor
Poverty	Affluence	Right	Wrong, left
Practicable	Impracticable	Rise	Fall
Practical	Impractical, theoretical	Rough	Smooth
		Sacred	Profane
Practice	Theory	Sad	Cheerful
Praise	Blame	Sanction	Disallow
Presence	Absence	Save	Spend
Proficient	Deficient	Scanty	Plentiful
Profit	Loss	Scold	Praise

Words	Antonyms	Words	Antonyms
Scorn	Reverse		durable
Sharp	Blunt, dull	Transparent	Opaque
Short	Long	Trivial	Important
Shy	Impudent	True	False
Simple	Complex	Uniform	Varied
Sink	Float	Unique	Common
Slow	Fast	Unite	Divide
Smile	Frown	Vacant	Full
Smooth	Rough	Vague	Definite
Soft	Hard	Verbal	Written
Sorrow	Joy	Vertical	Horizontal
Special	Ordinary	Vibrate	Petrify
Start	Stop	Vice	Virtue
Strange	Familiar	Victory	Defeat
Strong	Weak	View	Ignore
Sublime	Ridiculous	Violent	Gentle, quiet
Success	Failure	Vision	Blindness
Sufficient	Insufficient	Visitor	Host
Surrender	Victory	Vulgar	Refired
Sweet	Sour, bitter	Wakeful	Asleep
Swift	Slow	Want	Possess
Sympathy	Antipathy	Warm	Cool
Take	Give	Waste	Save, hoard
Tall	Short	Wavering	Steady
Tame	Wild	Wax	Wane
Teacher	Student	Wealth	Poverty
Teaching	Learning	Wet	Dry, arid
Tearful	Joyful	Whiten	Darken
Tedious	Lively	Wicked	Virtuous
Tenant	Landlord	Wide	Narrow
Tendency	Aversion	Wild	Tame, domestic
Tender	Strong	Win	Lose
Thankful	Thankless	Wonderful	Ordinary
Theory	Practice	Work	Repose, rest
Thick	Thin	Yield	Withhold
Timid	Fearless	Young	Old, aged
Top	Bottom	Youthful	Mature
Traditional	Modern	Zenith	Nadir
Transient	Lasting,	Zero	Numbers

B) Synonyms

A synonym is a word denoting the same meaning as another in the same language but suitable in different contexts or containing different emphasis. Synonyms are identical and coextensive in sense and usage with another word of the same language. Although they all have the same general meaning, each word has a special shade of meaning of its own. A list of words and their synonyms is as follows:

Words	Synonyms	Words	Synonyms
Abandon	Leave, forsake, give up	Alter	Change
		Amiable	Friendly
Abhor	Detest, hate	Anger	Rage, wrath, ire
Abnormal	Unusual, unnatural	Annual	Yearly
Abridge	Shorten, curtail, reduce	Anxious	Worried
		Appalling	Terrifying, dreadful, fearful
Absurd	Silly, ridiculous		
Abundant	Plentiful		
Achieve	Accomplish	Ask	Inquire
Acquiesce	Assent	Assistance	Help
Adept	Skilled, proficient	Attack	Assault
		Attractive	Pretty
Adequate	Sufficient	Aversion	Dislike
Admiration	Praise	Awful	Terrible, fearful
Admission	Entry	Barbarous	Uncivilised
Adoration	Worship	Base	Mean
Adversary	Enemy, opponent	Beginning	Start
		Behaviour	Conduct, demeanour
Adversity	Misfortune, calamity	Bias	Prejudice
Affection	Love	Blame	Accuse
Affliction	Sorrow, distress	Bliss	Happiness
		Boastful	Haughty
Affront	Insult	Bondage	Slavery
Aid	Help	Brave	Bold, courageous, venturesome
Alert	Watchful		
Alien	Foreign		
Allow	Permit, let	Brisk	Bright, lively vigorous
Almost	Nearly		
		Brutal	Cruel

Words	Synonyms	Words	Synonyms
Build	Construct	Courteous	Polite
Buy	Purchase	Crucial	Decisive,
Calm	Quiet,		critical
	tranquil	Cruel	Fierce,
Candid	Sincere, frank		tyrannical
Capture	Seize	Cure	Heal
Category	Class, group	Cynical	Misanthropic
Cause	Reason	Damage	Loss, harm,
Cautious	Careful,		injury
	punctilious	Damp	Moist
Chance	Opportunity	Deadly	Fatal,
Character	Nature		destructive
Choose	Select	Decay	Decline, wither,
Cite	Mention,		fade
	quote	Decorate	Adorn,
Clear	Distinct		embellish
Clumsy	Awkward	Decrease	Reduce
Coarse	Rough	Deficient	Lacking,
Coerce	Force, compel		inadequate
Common	Ordinary	Deformity	Malformation
Compassion	Pity,	Denounce	Accuse,
	sympathy		condemn
Compatible	Consistent	Deny	Refuse
Competition	Contest	Deplorable	Regrettable
Completely	Totally,	Design	Plan
	wholly, fully	Desire	Wish
Concise	Short, brief	Desolate	Lonely,
Condense	Compress,		deserted
	thick	Desperate	Hopeless
Confess	Admit	Destitute	Needy
Confident	Hopeful	Deteriorate	Degenerate,
Constancy	Steadfastness,		decline
	steadiness	Dexterity	Skill, deftness,
Contrary	Opposite		adroitness
Conversation	Talk	Didactic	Instructive
Cordial	Warm,	Diffident	Hesitant
	friendly	Diligent	Industrious,
Corrupt	Debased,		persevering
	tainted,	Disgrace	Dishonour
	depraved	Dismal	Gloomy

Words	Synonyms	Words	Synonyms
Display	Exhibit	Frankly	Openly,
Divine	Godlike,		honestly
	heavenly	Fraud	Deceit,
Donation	Contribution		trickery
Doubtful	Uncertain	Freedom	Liberty
Earnest	Serious	Frequently	Often
Earnings	Income	Fury	Anger
Eccentric	Odd	Fame	Reputation
Educate	Teach	Gaiety	Joyousness,
Efficiency	Ability		happiness,
Emergency	Exigency		mirth
Emphasise	Stress	Gentle	Kind, mild
Emulate	Imitate	Glance	Look
Endure	Tolerate	Gorgeous	Splendid
Energetic	Active	Grave	Sober, serious
Enormous	Huge	Grief	Sorrow, agony
Envy	Jealousy	Grievous	Painful,
Error	Mistake		sorrowful
Evidence	Proof	Guilt	Sin, crime
Exceptional	Unusual, rare	Habit	Practice,
Extravagant	Wasteful,		custom
	prodigal	Hamper	Hinder, impede
Fair	Beautiful, just	Hard	Difficult
False	Untrue,	Harm	Injury
	spurious	Hasty	Rash
Famous	Renowned	Hate	Dislike
Fanciful	Imaginative	Hinder	Obstruct
Ferocious	Fierce, savage,	Holy	Sacred
	barbarous	Humane	Kind,
Fertile	Productive		benevolent
Find	See, discover	Humble	Meek
Finish	Complete	Hunger	Starvation
Flimsy	Slight, thin	Hurt	Harm, injure
Foolish	Stupid, silly	Idea	Thought
Forgive	Pardon,	Idle	Lazy
	excuse	Illegal	Unlawful
Form	Make	Imagine	Think
Formerly	Previously	Immediately	Instantly
Frailty	Weakness	Imminent	Threatening
Frank	Candid, open		

Words	Synonyms	Words	Synonyms
Imperious	Authoritative	Love	Affection,
Imposter	Cheat		fondness
Inanimate	Lifeless, non-	Loyal	Faithful,
	living		devoted
Incessant	Continuous	Madness	Insanity, lunacy
Incite	Provoke	Magnificent	Splendid
Increase	Enlarge	Malady	Disease
Indignant	Angry	Malice	Spite, ill-will
Ingenuous	Artless,	Marriage	Matrimony,
	sincere		wedding
Innocuous	Harmless	Meagre	Small
Intention	Purpose	Mean	Low, abject
Jealous	Envious	Melancholy	Gloomy, sad
Jolly	Jovial, merry	Method	Manner,
Journey	Trip		mode
Jubilant	Joyful	Misery	Suffering
Judgement	Verdict	Mockery	Ridicule
Just	Fair, honest	Mourn	Lament
Juvenile	Youthful	Naive	Simple
Keen	Sharp	Nasty	Dirty, filthy
Kill	Murder,	Necessary	Essential
	assassinate,	Need	Necessity
	slay.	Negligent	Careless,
Kind	Charitable		needless
King	Monarch	Norm	Standard, rule,
Lament	Grieve,		principle
	mourn	Normal	Usual
Latent	Hidden,	Notorious	Infamous,
	dormant		wicked
Lax	Careless,	Novice	Beginner
	loose	Obscene	Indecent
Learning	Knowledge	Observe	Watch, remark
Leave	Depart	Obsolete	Antiquated,
Liberal	Generous		outdated
Liberty	Freedom,	Obstacle	Hindrance
	independence	Obvious	Evident, clear
Lie	Falsehood	Odd	Strange,
Likeness	Similarity,		peculiar
	resemblance	Odour	Smell
Lonely	Solitary	Old	Elderly

Words	Synonyms	Words	Synonyms
Opportune	Timely	Receive	Take, accept
Option	Choice	Recover	Regain
Ostensibly	Apparently	Refined	Elegant
Own	Possess	Reiterate	Repeat
Pardon	Forgive	Rejoice	Delight
Pathetic	Touching, moving, sorrowful	Relate	Describe, narrate
		Relevant	Pertinent
Pensive	Thoughtful	Remember	Recollect, recall
Permit	Allow		
Persuade	Urge	Remorse	Regret
Pious	Holy, devout	Renown	Fame
Pleasure	Satisfaction	Reside	Stay, live
Plentiful	Abundant	Respect	Regard, esteem
Polite	Courteous	Reticent	Reserved, silent
Portray	Draw, sketch	Revenge	Vengeance
Powerfully	Strongly	Riches	Wealth
Precise	Exact, systematic	Ruin	Destruction, downfall
Pretence	Pretext, excuse	Sacred	Holy, consecrated
Principle	Rule	Safe	Secure
Produce	Grow	Savage	Wild, barbarous
Proprietor	Owner		
Protect	Defend, save	Scandal	Infamy, slander
Prudent	Wise	Scanty	Slender, meagre
Quaint	Queer, odd		
Quake	Shake	Search	Seek
Quantum	Amount	Secret	Hidden
Queer	Strange, peculiar	See	Look, behold, stare
Quell	Suppress, subdue	Sense	Meaning
		Severe	Strict
Quench	Satisfy	Shame	Disgrace
Quest	Search	Shy	Bashful
Questionable	Doubtful, disputable	Similar	Alike
		Simple	Plain, natural
Radiant	Bright, brilliant	Sincere	Earnest, true
		Special	Particular
Rapid	Quick, fast		

Words	Synonyms	Words	Synonyms
Specimen	Sample	Vacant	Empty
Start	Begin	Vacation	Holiday
Sterile	Barren, unproductive	Vacillate	Waver
		Value	Worth, cost
Stiff	Rigid, stern	Various	Diverse, several
Strength	Power		
Subject	Topic, theme	Venom	Poison
Sublime	Elevated	Verdict	Judgement
Superficial	Shallow	Vigilance	Watchfulness
Surplus	Excess	Vindictive	Revengeful
Surround	Encircle	Voracious	Greedy
Tame	Mild, gentle	Vulgar	Coarse, crude
Tedious	Wearisome, monotonous	Wane	Decrease
		Warlike	Soldierly
Temporal	Worldly	Wasteful	Extravagant
Tender	Soft	Watch	Look, observe
Thankful	Grateful, obliged	Wax	Increase
		Wealthy	Rich
Theatrical	Dramatic	Weary	Tired
Thin	Lean, slim, slender	Wholesome	Healthy, sound
Thrifty	Economical	Wide	Broad
Thrive	Prosper, flourish	Will	Desire
		Wise	Prudent
Tired	Weary	Withstand	Resist
Tortuous	Winding	Wizard	Magician
Tradition	Custom	Wreck	Ruin, destroy
Ugly	Repulsive	Writer	Author
Unique	Single, unequalled	Yearn	Crave, desire
		Yield	Surrender, submit
Urbane	Polite, courteous	Zeal	Enthusiasm
Useful	Advantageous	Zenith	Top, summit
Usual	Common	Zest	Gusto

EXERCISES

1. Write the Antonyms of the following words:

   Humble, genuine, frank, freedom, enthusiasm, extravagant, arrogant, affluence, ambiguous, diligent, down, deficit, benevolence, benediction, languid, ingress, pardon, neat, miserly, remote, tendency, shy, scorn, queer, rash, sharp, unique, wax, vulgar, vague, transparent.

2. Write the Synonyms of the following words:

   Coerce, damp, category, guilt, fraud, dexterity, odd, melancholy, ingenuous, malady, mockery, savage, tedious, quake, plentiful, revenge, severe, temporal, yearn, urbane, wane, thrive, venom, imperious, magnificent, frank, flimsy, deteriorate, compatible.

13
INCHOATIVE VERBS

Inchoative verbs are those verbs which express the beginning, development or final stage of an action or state. Such words as 'get', 'become', 'grow', 'come', 'go', 'run', 'turn', 'wear' and 'fall' are called inchoative verbs. They may be used as follows:

a) Get

The word 'get' as an inchoative verb can be used with adjectives and their comparatives, and with participles used as adjectives. It is the commonest of the inchoative verbs and is very often used in colloquial English. It is also frequently used in progressive tenses and as such its construction is equivalent to 'become'; as,

   i) He is getting excited.
  ii) It's getting dark.
 iii) It's getting near breakfast time.
  iv) He is gradually getting weaker than before.
   v) He is getting his own way.
  vi) I do not get you.
 vii) Go and get your breakfast.
viii) Get me a ticket, please.
  ix) Please inform me as soon as you get here.

The word 'get' can also be used with 'to-infinitives'. When it is used in the simple past tense, it refers to the final stage of an action or state; as,

He is getting to be a good musician.
He didn't get to bed until 2 a.m.
Ramesh got to be Nirmal's intimate friend.
He gradually got to know the importance of your speech.
Where have they got to (what has become of them)?

Subhendu got the measles.

It is very often found that Mr. Das gets ill.

Sudhansu and Nikhilesh got to be good friends.

b) **Become**

The word 'become' as an inchoative verb, is normally used with adjectives and their comparatives, and with participles, used as adjectives; as,

i) He became jealous of me (grew, began to be).

ii) He has become accustomed to his new duties (got accustomed to).

iii) It's becoming much more expensive to travel abroad (getting).

iv) What will become of the children if their father dies (happen to)?

v) His new hat becomes him ? (be well suited to).

vi) He used vulgar language that doesn't become a man of his education (be right or fitting, befit).

vii) He became gaunt and weak (grew).

'Become' is not used with 'to-infinitives' and is not frequently used with prepositional phrases. But it can be used with nouns and in such cases, the indefinite article is normally preceded by the noun; as,

He became President of the Cooperative Societies of the Government.

He became a Director of the Food Corporation of India in 1966.

He soon became a man of extraordinary calibre.

He became an I.A.S. officer after his postgraduate studies.

c) **Grow**

The word 'grow' is normally used with adjectives and their comparatives, and with participles used as adjectives. It is also used with 'to-infinitives'; as,

i) The boy is growing taller.

ii) He is growing weaker.

iii) He was terribly afraid of that man and grew nervous.

iv) It's growing dark.

v) The weather suddenly grew cold.

vi) This boy is growing to be more and more like his father.

vii) He is growing to appreciate your behaviour.

d) Come

The word 'come' is normally used with adjectives and their comparatives, and with past participial adjectives denoting an undesirable or unsatisfactory state of action; as,

    i)   Your dream will one day come true.

   ii)   It comes easy with practice.

  iii)   The handle has come loose.

  iv)   It comes cheaper if you buy things in bulk.

   v)   Everything will come right in the end.

  vi)   That sort of thing comes natural to him.

 vii)   His shoelaces have come undone.

viii)   The flap of the envelope has come unstuck.

'Come' is also used with such prepositional phrases as, come of, come to, and with 'to-infinitives'; as,

That is what comes of being careless.

No good will come of it.

He comes of a good family.

He came to see that he was mistaken.

He had come to see the problem in a new light.

How did you come to be so foolish?

e) Go

The word 'go' is normally used with adjectives and with prepositional phrases.

    i)   He went blind at the age of 60.

   ii)   He went mad.

  iii)   Fish soon goes bad in hot weather.

  iv)   Ripe fruits quickly go rotten in hot weather.

   v)   He went red with anger.

  vi)   Ramanendra went pale at that shocking news.

 vii)   The Prime Minister's statement went a long way towards reassuring the nation.

viii)   The pistol didn't go off.

  ix)   This milk has gone off (has turned sour).

   x)   The milk went sour.

  xi)   The first prize went to Mr. Samarendra Das.

 xii)   Suresh went off his head.

f) Turn

This word can be used with adjectives and their comparatives. It can also be used with nouns without the use of an indefinite article, and with prepositional phrases; as,

  i)   These fruits are turning yellow.
 ii)   The milk has turned sour.
iii)   The weather has turned much hotter.
 iv)   He had to turn cook after the death of his wife.
  v)   We hope he will never turn Naxalite.
 vi)   It was really wise for that man to turn journalist.
vii)   The snow soon turned to rain.
viii) Water turns to ice when it freezes.

g) Wear

This word may be used with adjectives and their comparatives; as,

  i)   She never wears green.
 ii)   This material has worn thin.
iii)   The stone-steps have worn smooth!

h) Run

This word may be used with such adjectives as 'dry', 'low' and 'short'; as,

  i)   The tide is running strong.
 ii)   My blood ran cold.
iii)   The rivers are running dry.
 iv)   Supplies are running short.
  v)   Feelings ran high.
 vi)   The garden is running wild.
vii)   She lets her children run wild.

i) Fall

This word is normally used with adjectives. It is also used with 'to' and a noun or gerund to indicate the beginning of a state or action; as,

  i)   The arrow fell short.
 ii)   His horse fell lame.
iii)   He fell silent.
 iv)   He has fallen ill.
  v)   When does the rent fall due?
 vi)   The old man fell asleep.
vii)   I fell to wondering where to go for my holidays.

14
COURTESY, GREETING AND SALUTATION WORDS

The words 'please' and 'thank you' are normally used to express a sense of request and a sense of appreciation of a favour or kindness respectively. Such words as 'good morning', 'good evening', 'good afternoon', 'good night', 'goodbye', 'good day', etc. are normally used to express greetings and salutations. These courtesy words are used as follows:

a)   The word 'please'
i)   Expressing a polite form of request.

In expressing a polite form of request, the word 'please', may either be placed in the beginning of the sentence if the request takes the form of an imperative or at the end of a sentence if it bears the force of a request; as,

Would you hand over this watch to my friend, please?
Would you wait for me, please?
Come in, please.
Two coffees, please.
Please come in.
Please don't do that.
Please shut the door.

ii)   Expressing an offer or suggestion.

The word 'please' is used to express or accept an offer or suggestion and as such it implies a request; as,

Will you have another glass of milk?
Yes, please (or) no, please.

iii)   Taking the form of a question.

If the request takes the form of a question, the word 'please' may be used in the sentence. In this case it neither occupies the front position nor the end position in a sentence.

Will you please prevent your son from going there?
Will you please tell him about that matter?

b) **The words 'thank you'**
i) *Expressing appreciation of a favour or gratitude.*
Thank you for lending support to my brother at the time of trouble.
Thank you very much for the trouble you took for me.
Thank you for your help.
'Thank you' is the usual formula for 'I thank you'; 'No, thank you' is the formula used to decline an offer; 'thank you' is used for acceptance and may mean, 'yes, please.'
ii) *It is used in peremptory requests, usually with the future tense; as,*
I will thank you for that book.
I will thank you to be a little more polite.
iii) *Expressing an offer or suggestion.*
Is your tea sweet enough?
Yes, thank you.
Are you in need of my help?
No, thank you.

c) **Such words as 'good morning', 'good afternoon' *'good evening' 'good night' 'goodbye' 'good day'***
i) These words are normally used in forms of greeting and farewell; 'good morning' and 'good afternoon' are normally used either on meeting or on parting. 'Good evening' is usually said only on meeting but 'good night' is said on parting during evening hours, on retiring to bed for the night, on parting from friends at the end of the day, on greeting someone in the street but not stopping to speak to the person in the latter part of the evening.
ii) *Goodbye:* This word refers to farewell and is normally used between two friends or people on parting from each other. It is found that children use this form 'goodbye' for saying 'farewell' to other children of their age or even to grown-up people whom they know quite well. They prefer this term to 'good morning' or 'good afternoon'. For this purpose, schoolboys usually say 'Good afternoon, Sir,' to their teachers but 'goodbye' to their classmates. 'Good day' is not normally used in greeting and salutation. It is used for wishing some one well for the day.
iii) *Farewell:* This word is used in the sense of 'goodbye'. It is normally used in leave-taking.

□□□